CONFIDENT BABY CARE

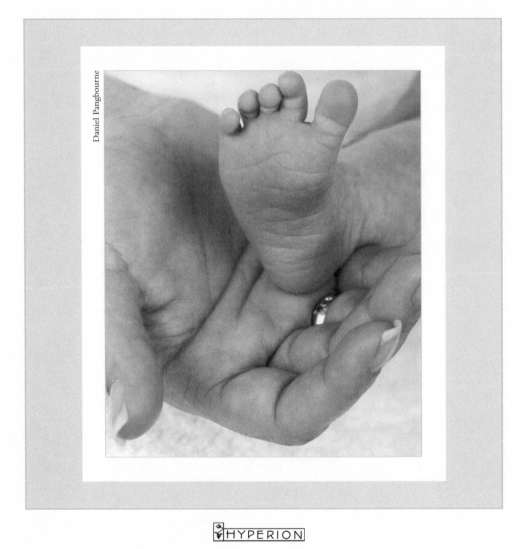

Daniel Pangbourne

HYPERION

N E W   Y O R K

CONFIDENT BABY CARE

What You Need to Know for the First Year
from America's Most Trusted Nanny

Daniel Pangbourne

JO FROST

ISBN: 978-1-4013-0906-0

Note to Reader:
The author has not purported to be qualified to give medical advice; nor is she giving medical advice. All information in the book concerning your child's health or development is for reference purposes only and is not intended to be used as a substitute for or to replace the advice of your physician or other qualified health professionals. The author and publisher specifically disclaim any liability arising directly or indirectly from the use of information in this book.

Hyperion books are available for special promotions and premiums. For details contact Michael Rentas, Proprietary Markets, Director, Inventory Operations, Hyperion, 77 West 66th Street, 12th floor, New York, New York 10023, or call 212-456-0133.

Design by Jo Anne Metsch

FIRST EDITION

10 9 8 7 6 5 4 3 2 1

This book is dedicated to YOU,

so that you have what you need right from the beginning

to help your baby grow into that loving adult.

◻

ACKNOWLEDGMENTS

A big thank you to:

*Mary Jane, for giving me clear direction
when there was always so much to say.*

*Love always to those closest to my heart, who continue to support me,
the work I do, and the truth behind it.*

*Daniel Pangbourne, the photographer, for creating the karma for such
wonderful images. Also thanks to Kevin Frazier for his contribution.*

*All the babies in the book: Jharrel (father and baby), Katie (bottle-feed),
Sherrall (sleeping), Chanel (gurgling), Olivia (eating), Joe (playing),
Riley (bath), twins: Teah and Sky, Keira and Kylie (reading),
Laura (hand and foot and newborn), Louis (cover). Not forgetting
Bijou, the pregnant model, and Greg in the father and baby shot.*

Hair and make-up stylist Tim Alan.

*Dr. Mark Furman at Great Ormond St. Hospital, London –
thanks for the thumbs up on the medical side of things.*

*Leslie Wells, thank you for your continued support and all at Hyperion
for delivering symbolically my baby.*

Jo Frost

MATTHEW FROST

Contents

PART 2   "B ABY'S HERE!" / 51

CONFIDENT BABY CARE

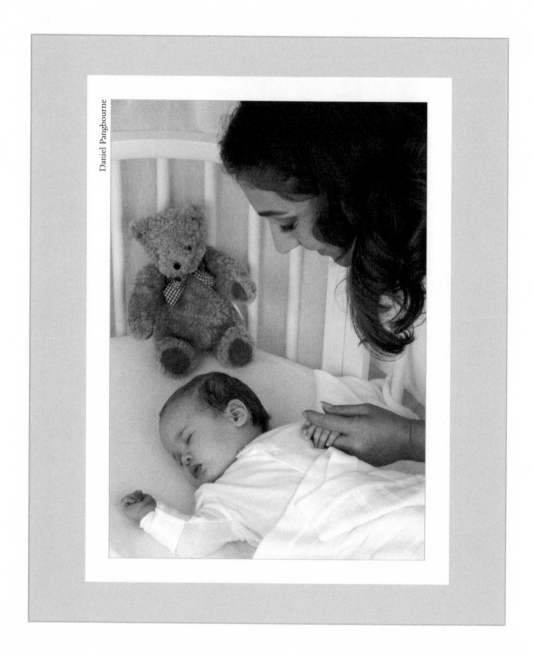

Daniel Pangbourne

Introduction

Congratulations! You're about to embark on the adventure of a lifetime—having a baby. To consciously raise a fine, well-adjusted child is the most serious commitment you will ever make in your life. You're about to bring forth new life—or, in some cases, new lives—and nurture a tiny being as he or she grows. But what makes this so exciting is that this isn't just the birth of your child, it is the birth of your family in this particular configuration. And, if this is your first, it's also the birth of you as a parent. Wow!

Recently I was with friends as they brought their newborn home from the hospital and was reminded again that all the planning in the world can't prepare you for the emotion and energy that your newborn will bring. Nothing can make you fully understand the feeling of holding your baby in your arms. You'll be experiencing this fabulous feeling for yourself very soon.

Naturally, however, you want to be prepared to be the best parent. So it's important to be as savvy as you can and read about how to make things go as smoothly as possible. That's why I've written this book—to give you the information you need to be the best parent you want to be. Keep it by your bedside so you can flip to it anytime you need as you go through your baby's first year, ready to help with any questions or concerns you might have. Think of it as your very own live-in me.

I've also written it for another important reason. No matter how many children you have, remember that this newborn is a miracle. That's where the saying "bundle of joy" comes from. It's kind of funny listening to people talk about babies. Over the years, I've noticed a lot of negativity about newborns—things like "Congratulations, you're not going to sleep for years"—and lots of advice about how to *cope. Cope* means you're in a situation that's a strain already.

My approach to baby care isn't about coping or dealing with strain. It's about helping you have the confidence to raise your baby in a healthy and content way. It's also about learning just who your baby is. For he has his own soul. Her own spirit. Your baby is a present, a gift of life itself, which will unfold and develop before your very own eyes.

While I've never had a baby, over the last seventeen years I've been with lots of families as they have brought their newborns home, and I know what a joyful, one-of-a-kind experience the first year can be when you've got the right attitudes, understanding, and equipment. Throughout my years as a nanny, I've had professors, psychologists, and pediatricians tell me that what they've studied for forty years, I've grasped "in the field." That's what I'll be sharing with you— my secrets from years of experience for making your baby's first year the wonder-filled celebration it was meant to be.

That's not to say you won't feel the rough as well as the smooth. There are going to be times when you feel exhausted or cranky, overwhelmed or worried. If I didn't say that, I wouldn't be honest with you. But that's all part of becoming a proud parent. Weathering the trials and tribulations along the way is how you learn. This book will help you iron out the wrinkles so that those moments are in the minority. Your baby, intuition, and I will be your guide. One thing to note—throughout this book, I alternate referring to a baby as he and she, as a way of acknowledging that there are both boys and girls.

Babies grow quickly and their needs change dramatically over the first year. That's why, after the initial chapters on getting prepared, I've broken most of the book into three-month sections. In each chapter, there's a section on:

- Development: the physical, mental, and social growth your baby will be going through over the year
- Babyproofing: what you need to do to assure your little one's safety
- Setting Firm Ground: routines, sleeping through the night, dealing with crying
- Feeding: all the how-to's, including establishing a feeding routine

- Parentcraft: dressing, bathing, diapering, burping, etc.
- Stimulation and Explorations: activities to help with mental, physical, and emotional development

Please understand that while the book is divided into 0–3 months, 3–6 months, 6–9 months, and 9–12 months, a baby is a living, breathing human being who grows and develops every day. So there aren't artificial cutoff points between one day and the next. What that means, for instance, is that as your baby turns three months old, you'll want to read up on the 3–6 month section, knowing that she is going at her own pace. I've also included a section for parents of babies in exceptional circumstances: multiples, preemies and other special needs, and adopted babies in which I discuss how you might need or want to modify my advice in other chapters to take your circumstances into account.

I'm a realist. Instead of just saying things like, "don't heat bottles in the microwave," or "don't use talcum powder," you'll be hearing the whys and the wherefores so that you can make the wisest choices possible. And when I feel something is absolutely crucial to do my way, you'll learn that too.

Since the journey is as much about you as your baby, each section also includes a chapter on your journey as a parent, for that will change too as you grow and develop. The first year is the time to create an all-important bond with your baby and set the foundation for positive parent-child interactions that will keep you from having behavior problems later. As parents, you'll learn to think on your feet, multitask, adapt to new challenges, and problem solve in a heartbeat. At any given moment, you'll be entertainer, teacher, nurse, bodyguard.

Because babies sense our feelings and experience them, one of the greatest gifts you can give your newborn is a sense of confidence in yourself. It's my hope that this book will give you the information and support you need in order to relax and trust yourself more and more.

Over the first year, you will come to love and grow with your child, who will be part of your life forever. May you treasure this precious time and your precious one who is coming into your life.

PART I

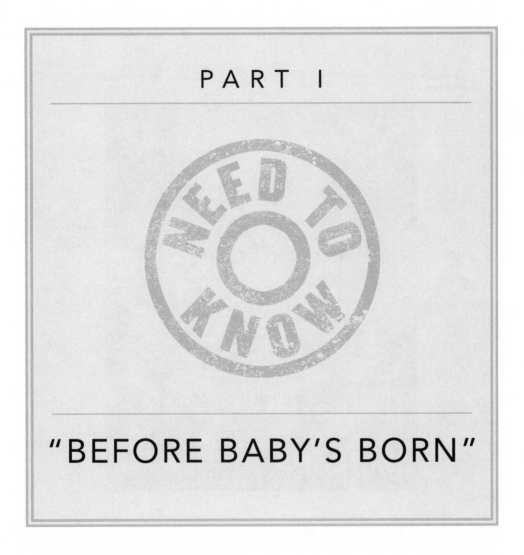

"BEFORE BABY'S BORN"

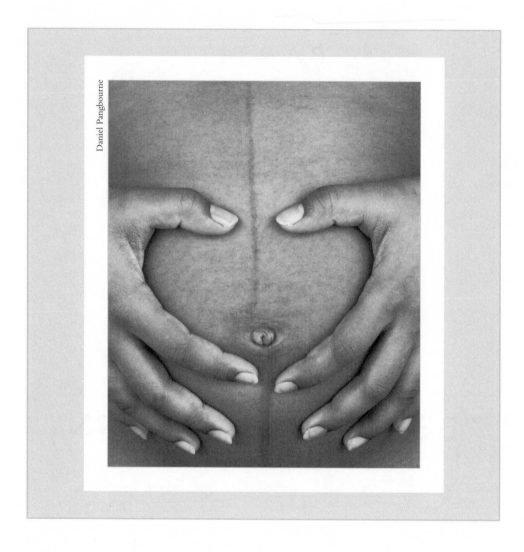

Daniel Pangbourne

CHAPTER 1

Becoming Confident Parents

hether this is your first or your fifth, when you have a baby, you're about to go on an emotional journey that is as unique as the two of you and this child. As any parent of more than one will tell you, no two babies are alike, and no two first years are alike for you or your baby. You may be full of intense feelings of love, or it may take time to bond with your newborn. You may get postnatal depression, or sail right through the hormone changes. You may feel exhausted and overwhelmed, or calm and joyful. Or all of the above on any given day. When you speak to other parents, and they say things like, "you'll never have sex again," "your house will be a mess," understand that they're talking about their own experiences. So try not to let others' expectations get in your way. Allow your experience to be just what it is. Unique.

What's also important to understand on this journey is that you may enjoy certain parts of it more than others. And that's okay. Each of the stages from 0–12 months will be very different and call on different skills. Some parents especially love the cuddly newborn stage; others can't wait for the more active times. Again, accept how both of you feel and understand that it's quite normal to experience this.

Some parents are very confident. Having a newborn feels like a brisk walk in the park. Other parents become really scared, unsure of what to expect, and worried they won't be able to cope. If you're feeling confident, that's a great gift to your partner. Confidence is contagious. If you feel a certain amount of vulnerability and awkwardness, don't be hard on yourself.

Anxious soon-to-be parents often ask me, "How will I know whether I'm doing it right, if I've never had a baby?" Here's what I always say: "You can't—and that's fine." Of course you can read and follow the guidelines in this book. They will help you a lot. But in the end, you can't know in advance what this particular baby is going to be like. You're going to find out along the way. It's on-the-job training! You'll learn that if you keep that diaper on too long, he's going to be uncomfortable and cry, so you change it sooner. You learn to read your child's facial expressions and sounds, recognizing, for instance, that maybe she's still hungry because she's crying in a particular way. Your baby tells you as you become more intuitive.

Remember—every other parent had to learn as they went along. Fortunately, while babies are vulnerable, they're also pretty sturdy beings. There are a few things you absolutely *must* do, such as support their necks, sleep them on their backs, keep them out of the sun. But if you don't put the diaper on right, put the little jumper on backward, or forget to burp him after a feed, it's not the end of the world. He'll soon let you know and you'll work it out!

Watching dads in particular, I've often noticed that the more they fragilely try to hold the baby, the more she cries because she senses his insecurity. Babies pick up our energy. That's what's special about babies: they have a sixth sense.

That's why I stress confident care. If you're very firm and confident as you pick up the baby and hold her as you'll learn in the section called Parentcraft, she'll sense your competency and be calm.

But as a first-time parent, that calm confidence can be very challenging. You may get overwhelmed, which can make you nervous and maybe not as mindful. So remember: slowly, slowly, gently, gently.

GROWING IN CONFIDENCE

I want you to learn how to make confident decisions. Confident decisions are decisions that you're happy with. Period.

As time goes on, your confidence will grow because you'll begin to see great results. This will help you to develop a knowing about what this child needs, and how to balance the needs of two or three if that's what you're learning this time. That inner knowing comes from the two of you listening to yourselves as well as your baby and other children. The more you pay attention to that inner voice, the more you'll learn to trust your instincts.

You'll also have more confidence because you've embraced your fears rather than run from them. I've met women who've been incredibly successful businesswomen and want to measure up in motherhood in the same successful way they did at work. I say why not. If you feel fearful right now, recognize that it's only an indication that you want to do your best—and that's wonderful! Any time you feel anxious, remember that it's a sign of wanting to do well and your wanting will *help* you do well. Visualize it being okay, you doing it well, your baby being happy . . .

You'll also grow in confidence because you'll come to understand that when you make the "wrong" decision, it isn't actually "wrong," because you've just learned from what you just did. You now know the correct way to do something. Confident parents make a decision, see what the outcome is, and then decide to make a better judgment next time if it wasn't the best choice. At some point, you'll have learned so much that you become absolute and wise about certain things. Because now you *know*. You don't think. You *know*.

That's why being a parent a second time is easier. If you're a second- or third-time parent, you might be thinking right now, "Well, but it's been five or six years, I've forgotten everything I learned when I had my first," don't worry. It's all in long-term memory ready to move into short-term. The actions will trigger the memory. As soon as the baby arrives, it triggers everything: "Ahhh, I remember!"

Parenting is about recognizing that the more you go on, the more you'll grow too. There are things that you did for your first child, for instance, that you don't want to do for your second child. Your opinions change and maybe your options too. You recognize that this child's temperament requires a different approach. You think about how to gel his personality with yours to build a relationship. That's what makes your relationship so special with each child that you have or the relationship that you have with your baby different from the one your partner has with him.

SECOND-TIME WORRIES

Second-time parents have a number of concerns. They wonder, "How can I possibly love another child as much as I love the child I have now?" As my mom and dad used to say, "Of course you can, your heart just gets bigger." You really can't know that until you experience it. But I know my brother, Matt, and I grew up feeling loved equally.

Second-timers may also worry about comparing the second with the first. Comparisons are inevitable, but keep them to yourself. You don't want either child to feel you're keeping score. You'll come to love what makes each unique. Especially those of you with twins (as you'll see later on).

Parents also reflect on balancing the needs of more than one child as well as themselves. You gave the first one all your love, attention, praise, and suddenly that is going to be halved. Will they be able to give each one what they need? Will they have time for themselves? These worries, like so many others, aren't anything you can really prepare for. You'll work it out as you go along. Focus on what you do well as a parent, or your worries only escalate. The routines in this book will help to find the balance for all.

SUPPORTING ONE ANOTHER

Because you're on a steep learning curve—whether that's about how to parent a newborn or how to integrate a newborn into your life with other children—loving support of one another is key. It's one of the things that make the difference in enjoying the first year or not.

Talk about your feelings. Relish the good feelings together and be emotionally open enough to express the feelings that are not so positive. When you speak about them to your partner, they don't fester and manifest in anxiety. Be there for one another; comfort one another when you need it with a hug or reassurance: "I feel really worried, and this baby's crying is really annoying me. I've become noise sensitive, I'm tired, and I'm irritable! And I'm tired! And I'm irritable." Many parents don't feel they can openly talk about their negative feelings because they think it's an indication of failing when they've only just begun. But when you talk about it, your feelings are out there to be dealt with. So be understanding and compassionate with yourself and each other. Then move on to resolving these issues *together*. As much as health visitors and GPs are there to answer questions, they are not living with you. So as a partner, if you see your wife or husband struggling, reach out, don't ignore.

REACHING OUT TO OTHERS

Allow this baby to make the family circle together. Relatives, especially grandparents, have a very special role in your new family dynamic. Hopefully they will be there to support the two of you and develop that special bond with your child as well. Allow them to enjoy the experience of being grandparents by making time for them to connect with your newborn. I've seen grandparents who say, "Oh thank God, it's about time!" And some respond, "Oh, I'm too young to be a grandparent!" How much they are involved depends a lot on their own circumstances. Maybe you're having that baby boy among all the girl grandkids. Already Granddad's giving him a fishing rod and he's not even born yet. Or your baby is their sixth grandchild so they're pretty ho-hum, but will always be excited about being the grandparents of six. Whatever is true for them, get clear between the two of you what you would like from them in terms of support, and make your wishes clear. Ask them to do the same. It will change throughout the first year, but don't say anything till at least the third month unless your parents are the co-carers too.

Connect with other parents as well. It's so important to hear how other parents are feeling and share learning. In the past, when we lived in extended families, we were given reassurance from parents, aunties, sisters, and others around us who had children. They all said, "It will be fine." We leaned on their reassurance to pull us through to the next stage. Now we often live so far apart that we can't rely on them on a daily basis. That's why connecting with other parents can be so helpful mentally and emotionally. The Internet too is a good source of information to ease worries. My Web site (which you can find in the resource guide in the back) has been very successful, like others I'm sure.

There are all sorts of wonderful groups out there. You may have connected already with folks from your prenatal classes. If not, you can find a group through the resource guide in the back of this book.

It's important that the people surrounding you give support that's reassuring and allows you to grow. I've seen mothers and fathers who want to learn, but are surrounded by friends and relatives who are critical and judgmental.

This can be particularly problematic for new mothers. At a time when you feel vulnerable because you've just had a baby, your hormones are all over the place, and you're anxious because you want to make the right decisions, your vulnerability may leave you open to self-doubt. So that if somebody says something negative, whereas before you might think, "No, actually I'm going to do this," you question and doubt yourself. And if you start to doubt, you leave things too open, and that's not good for you or your baby. So be sure to seek support that *is* supportive, and don't be afraid to keep your distance from anyone who makes you doubt your parenting abilities. We don't want you to feel intimidated.

Let me reassure you too. I'm the nanny on your shoulder, here not only to give you practical advice, but to nurture and support you on your journey during this first year. I want you both to have that glow, that warmth inside that gets generated when you feel proud about yourself as a parent.

Since I was very young, I've been drawn to babies and children, and vice versa. I was the child in the swimming pool on vacation who met all the kids. I've always had a strong intuition about babies and kids. As a nanny, I listen to my intuition, as you will learn to do, and also pay attention to what's working and not. That's why I get good results. Throughout these pages, I will be offering you suggestions that I know work. The success you'll achieve will grow your confidence, just as it did for me.

THINK POSITIVELY

Whether this is your first or not, I believe strongly in having a positive attitude. That's because it increases the likelihood of a good outcome. Studies show, for instance, that if you expect that your baby will keep you up all night, she does. If you *expect* that she's going to sleep well, that happens more frequently. So expect the best and don't look for problems. That's not to say you should ignore the ones that are there—just don't go looking. And when things don't turn out as expected, deal with it without magnifying the problem even more with your worries. You have neither the time nor energy.

Many women have birth worries—will it hurt too much? Will they be able to do it? Will the baby be okay? It's fear of the unknown. This is definitely a time to feel the fear and do it anyway. Because you are going to give birth, one way or another.

I always tell women to stay away from people who are full of negativity about giving birth. It's important to have people to tell you birthing stories that are realistic. But I know women who go on the Internet to find out about one thing and end up freaking themselves out about birthing situations. Don't borrow trouble. No need for drama.

This is not to say that things never happen. Rather, I'm encouraging you to have a positive mind-set with regards to bringing your newborn into the world. There's a lot to be said for having happy thoughts and doing the things that support you in your pregnancy, and being surrounded by people who are positive. That way, the happy chemicals are released and you feel good.

Remember, you do have a choice to avoid negative people and think positively. You have that choice, period.

Part of being positive is focusing on what you want, not on what you don't want. For instance, second timers often say to me, "I don't want the older to be jealous. I don't want them to not get along. I don't want to be overwhelmed." Okay, I say, what *do* you want and how are you going to achieve it? Talk together about how to get the results you want: We want our children to get along. How can we make that happen? Then make those first steps.

WHAT KIND OF PARENT DO YOU WANT TO BE?

Unfortunately, we can very easily find the kind of parents we don't want to be. We're very quick to point the big index finger at who we don't want to be. That's why I think it's very important for soon-to-be parents to talk together about what kind of parents they want to be. Not all of us have had the best examples, and we need to be as conscious as possible about choosing how we're going to behave in this new role.

I suggest you each sit down with a pad of paper and a pen and fill in this sentence: "I want to be a parent who . . ." Here are some examples:

- understands my children
- teaches them my values
- loves unconditionally
- shows them what a loving relationship is
- accepts my children for who they are
- has energy
- has fun
- is there for them
- is there for them as much as my partner is

Then compare your two lists and ask yourselves, how are we going to get the results we want?

Do this exercise before going to the next chapter. Because the clearer you can be about what's important to you, the easier it will be to make the decisions you need to make before your baby's birth. Your answers will help you think about the important choices we'll explore in the next chapter.

COORDINATING PARENTING STYLES AND TASKS

One thing you need to understand is that each of you is going to have a unique parenting style. You create a fashion style by combining different pieces together to give you individuality. Similarly, how you approach these elements in the book is what will give you your own unique parenting style. Your approach may be less concerned, for instance, around babyproofing with toilet lid locks than other parents, because you understand your baby's nature and know where you need to be very assertive when it comes to safety. Your particular choices make up your style.

While each of you is going to have a unique style, it's important to come together and compromise about key issues. Otherwise, it can end up that one parent feels undermined.

So talk about your parenting philosophies. What about discipline? Character building—raising a child who is moral and socially responsible? How will you come together? What happens when you disagree? Are you both willing to enforce routines? While a lot of issues won't arise until the second year and you can't know all of this in advance, it's important to create as much of a sound foundation of agreement as possible right at the start. You're going to read my advice, but ultimately you will need to decide what to do. And it's best if you're in general agreement for everyone's sake.

This doesn't mean you're going to have one conversation and be done. You'll need to be checking in with one another as you go along and different situations arise. But right now, before the baby's born, I want you to really communicate with one another, to get on the same page from the beginning.

These conversations may raise issues from your own upbringing. What do you want to carry into your family's life and what do you want to leave behind? A lot of the behavior stuff that I dealt with families about is a result of unexamined things they bring from their own childhood. As a result, they begin to question their upbringing. But they already have children of their own.

I want you to start looking at these things *before* you have the baby. So you can go into this experience with a level of maturity and awareness. So that you do things because you know they're right, not just because as a parent yourself, you can.

Of course you can't know in advance all of what will be triggered from your own past. But the more you're aware, the better choices you'll make. That's why it's so important that you challenge yourselves to ask one another those tough questions. Because you've made a decision to raise a child together in a complex society where there are all sorts of conflicting advice. The challenge is for you to *continue* making conscious decisions together. Because this is not just about having a baby. This is a responsibility and a commitment for life that you have to stand up and be counted for. I know you can do it because you want to. Otherwise you wouldn't be reading this book.

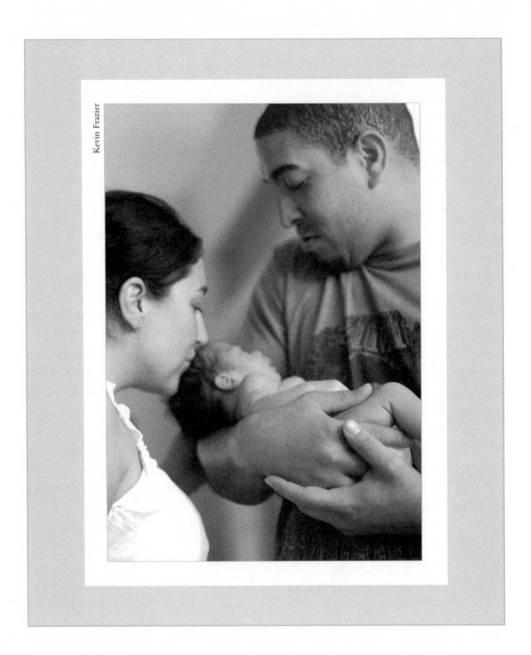
Kevin Frazier

CHAPTER 2

Making Confident First Choices

hen you first met your partner, you spent time getting to know one another. You dated and talked and fell in love. At some point you made the decision to commit to one another, which is one of the biggest commitments you'll ever make in your life. Then you make a commitment to have a child together, which is the other big life commitment, and suddenly you stop talking about the important things.

I see this all the time with the families I work with. Couples discuss what kinds of vacations to take, how to decorate the house, where to go on the weekend. But they don't take the time to get on the same page with one another on the crucial issues about raising their child. Breast-feeding, sleep schedules, discipline, day care, grandparents, dealing with other children—all the issues they are going to encounter. Even when they focus on having a baby, it's easy for people to get lost in what color the nursery's going to be and forget the fundamentals. Quite frankly, it doesn't really matter what color paint is on the wall. What really matters is parenting a happy, healthy child. And to do that, you need to make decisions as a couple about how you're going to raise this baby who's about to be born.

So knuckle down now and have those important conversations before the birth: What should we name our baby? How do you feel about breast-feeding? What's your take on how, as a father, you're going to be involved? What kind of help are you going to need in the first few weeks and beyond? Will Dad take paternity leave? How long is Mom going to be on maternity leave? You usually go on vacation at Christmas. Your baby is being born in September. Does that mean you'll be at home for Christmas this year? Think things through.

Of course, you can never be prepared to answer everything 100 percent, but the more you do prepare in advance, the more in control you'll feel, even if things don't all work out as you planned. Preparation means you won't be in such a hectic situation after the baby's born, trying to work all these things out. Preparation also helps stop worries playing in your head day in and day out so they don't magnify.

In the last chapter, I spoke of becoming confident parents. Part of that is understanding that confident choices are *your* choices. You should be making the best decisions you can for you and your family, not to please your in-laws, your friends, or your mother, even when you feel tempted. Of course, that's not to say you never listen to advice. But when you're about to have a baby, friends, family, and even strangers tend to offer their pennies' worth about what you should and shouldn't do. All of this advice can be overwhelming, and you can feel pressured into doing things you don't agree with. Follow your gut. Thank the other person for caring and let them know you are going to do what you think is best. Take bits of advice from here and there, and then make your own decisions.

The rest of this chapter will give you an idea of the things you should be considering, as well as my perspective on what works best. Have these conversations and plan well in advance!

NAMING YOUR BABY

Nothing is both more fun and full of issues than coming up with a name for your baby. The most important thing here is that the two of you pick something you both like. This may take a lot of back-and-forth. Put any top candidates through Jo's naming test:

- How does it sound with your last name? Do the initials spell something you wouldn't want to say?
- What kind of nickname comes with this name? Kids can be pretty cruel, and it will get abbreviated.

- Can it grow with your child? Some names are great for babies but don't work as the child grows. Or vice versa.
- Imagine calling the name out in a crowd. Do you feel silly or pretentious?
- Is it as glam as the life you lead?

Now that you've driven yourselves mad and finally found a name you can both agree on, you may want to keep your choice to yourself until after the baby's born. Because once you announce it to the world, you're going to hear everyone's opinion of your choice. This can definitely be a hot-button family issue.

Some parents wait until the baby's born to make their final choice. Or perhaps you'll change your mind on the day. It wouldn't be the first time after the birth that there have been *X*'s floating around the wards. That's fine too.

PREPARING TO GO TO THE HOSPITAL

Make sure your suitcase is ready and that you've got the first set of baby clothes laundered and ready to go. I hope you also have created a system for laundry, washing, shopping, and other household tasks. If not right now, at least get something started by the first month to get you up and running again. These tasks can be organized so that they're done on certain days. You want to make as easy a routine as possible.

Make a delivery plan. Who's taking Mom to the hospital? Where's Dad going to be? Who's going to mind the other kids while you're gone? How about the pets?

Have backup plans. What if he can't make it in time? Who can you call if you can't reach the kids' minder? Do you have the number of the local

NEED TO KNOW

FOOD PREP

You want to minimize cooking and shopping duties. So stock up the fridge just before you go to the hospital and cook as many meals as you can and freeze them for the other kids. You'll be happy you did when you can just pop one into the microwave and serve. Or get delivery set up for when baby's born. In other words, chill . . .

car/taxi service? Remember, this baby may not come on schedule. And if you don't get it done, oh well, it's going to happen anyway because let's face it, the baby comes when he comes!

FATHERS' ROLE

I strongly support the movement to have fathers more involved in the day-to-day care of their newborns. It's important to involve them from the very beginning for two reasons. First, so that they can begin to bond with the baby and learn how to be confident dads. Second, so that the couple can feel together in the experience rather than mothers feeling overwhelmed and fathers feeling alienated or pushed to the side. In order to do this, mothers need to recognize that wearing the martyr crown—only *I* can do this—is going to lead to sleep deprivation and loss of an ability to produce breast milk.

From speaking to dads who are now fiftysomething, and were in their early forties when they had kids, many felt a little bit pushed to the side in the beginning and had to learn to jump in and take an active role. They grew up with "it's the woman's role." Many younger dads now feel comfortable from the very beginning and really help create a fifty-fifty partnership.

We're long past the days when child rearing was considered women's work. Get clear on Dad's role. This will influence decisions you make in this chapter about after-birth help, breast-feeding, time off, etc. And you read through the rest of the book together, stop and ask yourselves in each chapter, which one of us will take this part on? Or, who will do what, when? Make it easier for yourselves.

CREATING A POSITIVE EXPERIENCE FOR OLDER CHILDREN

Second timers ask me all the time about when they should tell their firstborn that Mommy's pregnant. I think it really depends on the age. If there's a five- or six-year gap between the older and newborn, then you can explain a lot of what is going to happen. But remember, even kids this age don't really have a concept of time. I would leave discussing it until you're protruding right out. Of course, if he starts asking questions, then answer: "We're having a baby. You're going to be a big brother." Just as with yourselves, emphasize the positive.

Really young children don't really understand the meaning of events like births. Their feelings are created by noticing the response of the people around them. The more you make it a big, happy adventure that she's going to be a big sister, the more she'll respond positively and know this is a good thing.

I always advise buying a dolly with baby clothes, basket, and bath, etc. so he can take care of his baby while you're taking care of yours. Allow toddlers to do jobs so that they feel they're a part of what you're doing: "Can you please get me a blanket for the baby? She needs our help." For older children in the pre-teens, well, it's all about them chipping in too.

If your child is younger, it really is about dealing with things on the hop when they happen. If there's only eighteen or twenty months between the two, you're probably sitting there thinking, How am I going to manage two when they both need to be changed? Or put to bed?

I assure you that you will work it out. I actually like the idea of having children close together. In the beginning, it may give you a few more gray hairs (only joking—by now you're probably dying for a cut, color, and blow-dry). But when they get a bit older, they'll be able to be great companions to one another. When it comes to the first year, recognize that you must deal first with the needs of the baby and then your other child. Yes, it's a juggling act, but you'll get better with practice.

You need to use your judgment as to whether your firstborn should come to the hospital and see you in an unfamiliar environment, with the baby by your side. It depends on what will make you more comfortable and on what kind of child she is. I've seen kids who want to climb up into the incubator and then parents start worrying so they sharpen their tone a bit more than they would at home. Parents, child, and baby end up agitated and upset.

When I'm with a family who's just had a baby, I usually help the older ones celebrate the birth back at home by blowing up balloons and saying excitedly, "Mommy's having a baby right now! And you're a big sister!" It's a party, a big celebration.

I feel very strongly about not off-loading the older child to Grandma's for a week because of the birth. Step up to the challenge of your new family configuration. Otherwise your firstborn will feel displaced. Keep your child in his home, and bring the new baby into the situation. You may need more help in order to care for the newborn, recover physically yourself, and give your older child the attention he needs. That's fine. But have the help come to you.

In advance, think about your older child's activities. When your child needs to go to activity classes and you've got the newborn, what are you going to do? If possible, it's great to continue to maintain the routine. But if that's not possible, don't beat yourself up. The point is to have time after the birth filled with the maximum of joy. You can start up all the groups again in a few weeks' time.

TO BREAST-FEED OR NOT

There are important health benefits to breast-feeding. Breast milk contains the right combination of fat, protein, carbohydrates, vitamins, and minerals for infants, plus antibodies, which boosts your baby's immune system at the time when she is most vulnerable to illnesses. It has also been shown to reduce gas and constipation. Even a few weeks of breast-feeding helps give your baby a healthy start.

There are a few other advantages—it's free and you don't have to mess with bottles, powder, etc. Plus it also burns off calories (making it easier to get back to your pre-pregnancy weight) and produces a hormone called *prolactin*, which creates a feeling of well-being and calm.

I definitely support breast-feeding, but not to the extent of making bottle-feeding parents feel they should be banished off the face of the earth. There are a variety of reasons you may not be able to, including adoption, illness, and certain medications. I know women who can't breast-feed because their nipples are inverted or too short. It's okay if you can't or choose not to. Remember— generations of babies were bottle-fed and are just fine! Formula is now created to mimic breast milk closely (minus the antibodies).

So don't feel badly, Mom, if for some reason you can't breast-feed or you do it only for a few weeks. It's not proof of your womanhood or of your love for your baby. And women, be kind to other moms who are not breast-feeding. Support one another, rather than judge!

At the end of the day, whether you choose to breast-feed or not, what's fine is the decision you made. Parenting means making all kinds of decisions based on your needs and circumstances, as well as the needs of your child. I want you to make the best choices you can, without feeling pressure from others, and then stand comfortably in your choice.

You can also choose, as friends of mine recently did, to pump milk and bottle-feed so that both of you can share equally in feedings. How nice! Dad can help and Mom can get more sleep. It's a lovely idea, but be aware that Mom probably won't sleep, at least not at first. Because when that baby cries to be fed, your breasts are probably going to go, "Feed the baby, feed the baby, feed the baby." They're going to feel like hot watermelons! Most likely you're going to be torn between letting your husband give that bottle and your boobs saying, "Give me release. Give me release!" So don't feel badly if it doesn't work out as you planned.

If you do think you might want to breast-feed, even for a short while, decide before your baby is born. Because he's going to be hungry, and you'll want to latch him on as soon as possible to stimulate the flow.

SLEEPING ARRANGEMENTS

Another thing to work out is where your baby is going to sleep. Some people have the nursery already. They've decked it all out and only need the baby to *complete* the room! I would strongly suggest you hold back on putting your baby in another room. He should be with you.

In the beginning, you're going to be feeding on demand. To be honest, if you can save yourself getting out of bed and walking into another room by just reaching over and putting the baby on you, all the better. You'll also want to be near your baby in the beginning, just to make sure he's breathing. All parents do this. You're going to be checking frequently to know he's safe: "Let me make sure it's all the same from when I last looked ten minutes ago." That's why I don't suggest that you put them in another room until they're at least four months. At least. Nearest is best.

This is particularly important if you have other children, because older children are curious. They may want to jump in to have a sleep with the baby. If the baby is by your side, you can make sure that doesn't happen, and explain there'll be plenty of time to do this when their sibling is older.

IMMUNIZATIONS

Recently there has been a lot of publicity about whether to give babies certain immunizations. I feel absolutely that you must give your child all of them and on the recommended schedule. Don't question, just protect your child.

Here's why. Despite all the news, there are no hard-core facts that certain immunizations cause autism or any other diseases. But we do know with 100 percent certainty that immunizations prevent deadly childhood diseases. We're seeing outbreaks of measles, chicken pox, whooping cough, and other diseases because people are choosing not to immunize their children. Immunizations exist to prevent your child from having diseases that can cripple, that can blind, that can deform and *kill*. Don't mess about with this!

STORING CORD BLOOD

Some parents these days are choosing to store their newborn's umbilical cord blood to be used in case she later develops certain cancers, blood or genetic disorders, or to be used for sick siblings. The science of this is new, and there are no estimates on the likelihood of needing this blood. If this is something you are interested in, particularly if your family has any medical history where transplants have been required, discuss this with your doctor before the birth, as it must be done right after birth.

CIRCUMCISION

Circumcision is the removal of the foreskin at the top of the penis, which then exposes the tip (called the *glans*). Unless you're doing it for religious reasons so there is no question about it, I believe this choice needs to be an informed decision that you make with your doctor's advice. Here are the medical facts as we currently know them. Circumcision:

- Reduces the risk of urinary tract infections by 3.7 times
- Reduces the risk of skin inflammation and a disorder called *paraphimosis,* which is when the foreskin gets stuck when it's first retracted
- May reduce the risk of penile cancer and sexually transmitted diseases
- Causes complications in one of 476 cases. Bleeding and minor infections are the most common, but severe damage can occur.

If you choose to do it, it's recommended that it be done in the first three days of life and only on healthy, full-term babies (preemies should wait until they're stable and grown a bit). I do know children who have had trouble with infection and had to be circumcised later, even as late as in their teens.

In addition to medical or religious considerations, you may take other factors into account. For instance, maybe Daddy's not circumcised and you want your son to be similar. It's a personal choice the two of you will make.

CHOOSING A PEDIATRICIAN

Picking the right doctor for your baby is crucial for your peace of mind. The best way is to get recommendations from friends and family. Your obstetrician can also make recommendations. Both of you should interview three or so, and choose before your baby's born. You're looking not only for someone who's well qualified and takes your health insurance, but who you feel comfortable talking with and asking "dumb" questions. You are going to see a lot of this person, beginning with a visit at the hospital during the first twenty-four hours, then regular checkups at one, two, four, six, nine, twelve, fifteen, eighteen, and twenty-four months, then yearly afterward, as well as any sick care. You want to feel that he or she takes your concerns seriously and is there to help you in your new role. You want to make sure you're comfortable with his or her philosophy of child rearing. How is her manner with kids? Can you imagine your child being comfortable with him? Here are some basic questions:

- What are the office hours?
- What's the procedure for after-office emergencies?
- When is the doctor available to speak to and how—e-mail? Phone?
- Who covers when he or she is not there?

Remember, you can always change if you end up not finding this person responsive to you or your child's needs.

STOPPING WORK

How much time you should take off in advance of the birth depends on your finances, your maternity and paternity leave, and Mom's medical condition. I know many women have worked right up until the last minute due to financial concerns. I know others who have decided to take the luxury of a month off before the birth because they wanted to nest. This is something that you work out between you two, given your circumstances.

Understand that this decision may be forced, depending on the condition of your pregnancy. If you've had a rough ride, you might suddenly need to have an easy month because the pregnancy's becoming more and more tiresome. Or if you get preeclampsia and your blood pressure's going up and your ankles are swollen, you're putting yourself and your baby at extreme danger if you don't get off your feet. Or you're ordered to have complete bed rest so you won't deliver prematurely. Under those circumstances, you end up leaving before you planned and have to deal with that.

AFTER-BIRTH HELP

It's important to think about this issue in two ways because your baby's needs (and the new mom's) are more intense in the very beginning:

- What kind of support system are you going to put in place for right after the birth?
- If you both work outside the home, how are you going to maximize

time off to spend with the baby in the first few months? (We'll look at finding help after going back to work in the next section.)

Let's start with the first time frame. Mom, don't underestimate the emotional, physical, and mental changes that occur once you give birth. It's important that you have a lot of loving support right after the birth. They don't call it "labor" for nothing. Whether you've given birth vaginally or via Cesarean, your body has just gone though an extreme ordeal, and needs time and rest to mend. Some women just pop out those babies. I salute those who do! But many women feel like they've been dragged through a bush backward. Not to mention the hormonal shifts and possible feelings of anxiety over handling everything. You're going to need an extra pair of hands, whether that's to spell you to take a shower, soothe a colicky baby, cook a meal, take the toddler for a walk, or share how you're feeling and work through what you're learning. You also want to have a lot of time in the first few days just to lie around with your baby.

Some people are very lucky to have many folks around them to give them that cushion. Others just have their partners. If you have a positive relationship, having your mom, sis, auntie, or best friend as your maternity helper is the best. Check in with them as early as possible to see if they can arrange to be there around your due date. People's lives are so complicated that the more advance notice the better.

If that's not possible and you can afford it, having a doula or nanny is also wonderful because they have so much experience. This is what I did for many families. Doulas are specially trained helpers in the emotional journey of giving birth and the transition to parenthood. Some help parents during the birth process itself; others come in after to give guidance and increase your self-confidence. The resource guide in the back will help you find one if it seems appropriate.

You can also consider an au pair or mother's helper during the day. They can't have sole responsibility for a baby or other children, but they can offer help at a lower cost than a nanny. A cleaning person may also be a godsend for domestic chores.

Talk with your partner about the best time for Dad to be there. If it's just the two of you, can he take a few weeks off to be with you? Mostly like, he's going to *want* to be around for himself as well as you. Think about it together in the context of the other support *you've* got. If your mom or auntie is there in the beginning, then some fathers feel like, "I'll come in on the second week because we're going to be bombarded with estrogen the first week!"

It all depends, really, on how the two of you are feeling. Tell one another the honest truth and find a way to meet both your needs. Because even if her mom's coming around, she may really want you, her partner, by her side that first week. So take emotional considerations into account as well as what makes sense practically.

If you both work, you also need to think about how much time to take off. Whether you qualify for paid leave and for how long depend on the size of the company you work for and the state you live in. Find out your employer's policy. If your employer is not covered under the Family and Medical Leave Act or state law, you may be able to strike a deal for yourself. Find out what they've done for others, get it in writing, and make sure your boss and whoever is in charge of HR gets a copy.

Some parents stretch out the time by adding on their vacation time to their paid leave. However you work it out, your number-one priority should be for Mom to take as much time off as possible during that first year. I also know people who have stretched out parental care for the baby by one parent taking

NANNY KNOW-HOW: CALM FIRST WEEKS

Once you give birth, all your friends and relatives are going to want to come by and see the new baby. Aside from your designated helpers and your immediate family, I suggest you have people come *after* the first week or so if they want to stay for a while. You need time to physically recover, adjust to your newborn's needs, and bond. Your baby needs time to get used to the stimulating world. Plus, you both would do better without a parade of germs. Get acquainted with one another and then invite others in. Give yourself calm and quiet. Use your phone answering machine. Let Dad post a baby page online to keep relatives informed and the calls down. If you are being bombarded with people wanting to visit, at least create visiting hours so that you confine it to a set time of day. True friends will abide by your wishes.

several months off, and then the other. If you consider doing that, I suggest Dad taking the later months rather than the first. This gives Mom an opportunity to breast-feed and be home when the baby is tiny. Then she can express milk for Dad to do the feedings or switch to formula.

GOING BACK TO WORK

For some, Mom will not be a full-time mother and housewife. So the day will come when you'll go back to work. This is a huge transition, which mothers often find very challenging. It can feel like you're doing the wrong thing, no matter what the age of your child.

Having to go back to work or choosing to go back is very different. If you have a choice, I believe this is not a decision that you will be able to 100 percent make until after your baby's born. You can think now, "This is what I'm going to do," and when you've had that baby, you may think, "No way." So you find a way to go back part-time. Or take more time off.

Not all women have that choice. Some of us have to go back to work when our babies are very young.

Whether you have to go to work or choose to, before you step foot out that door, you must find someone whom you *completely*, completely trust on *every, every* level to leave your baby with. Your first priority is your child. You'll deal with your emotions when you deal with them and I'll help you when you get to that part of the journey. You've got to have absolute trust that you're leaving the most precious person in your life with someone who can be counted on totally. Otherwise, how will you function? You won't . . . that's your baby!

Because it's such an important decision, I suggest parents give themselves plenty of time to find the right solution. Begin by taking a realistic look at your circumstances. Will you be going back full- or part-time? Are you on a regular work schedule, or do you often work late or need to go in early? Then, based on that information, plus finances, make a decision given the available choices. There are basically four options, each with its own pros and cons, including cost:

- Family members
- Nanny or nanny share

- Day care center with lots of other children
- Private home of a child minder with a couple other babies or children.

FAMILY

A lot of people have a family member care for their baby not only because they're family but because it's free. If you choose this option, be sure never to take advantage of your family. Because you have a need and they're a great solution, there's a tendency to lean on our relatives and then have repercussions down the line. Just because she's your mom or granny, don't take her for granted. Let her know all the time how thankful you are and don't ask for more and more time. I've seen single parents in particular take advantage. Without really realizing it, they often put too much burden on the co-carer.

Also, be realistic. Can this person really care for your infant every day, all day? Over and over, I've seen family members who say, "Oh, it would be fine!" and five months down the line realize it's too much for them. I've gone into many families where the grandma says to me, "I feel bad, but I don't want to look after my grandson because I'm worn-out. I can't do it anymore." They feel guilty and are afraid to tell their daughter or son. So I end up doing it.

That's why I think it's important to say, "Let's start off with two or three months and see how it goes because I don't want it to be a burden on you." Then expect that there may be changes. Keep an open relationship—talk about how it's going and how each of you is feeling. Also, if you can afford it, consider giving them a little token of your appreciation. If they don't accept, then fine.

Also, to avoid any wrinkles, be clear up front in the nicest possible way what you're asking her to do in terms of routines, etc., and ask if she's willing to follow that. Let's not mistake, your mother earned the right to turn around and say, "I raised you and your brother and so I know what to do." But in general, the person you choose has to respect what you two want for your child. If the person you're considering is very controlling and not likely to respect your wishes, you might want to try to find someone else.

There's an unhealthy liberty I've seen a relative co-carer take, when she does it her way because she knows you need her. That's awful because it puts the parent in a really sticky spot because they desperately need the help. I would encourage you to avoid that situation if at all possible and, if you find yourself in it, to get out right away! Not only will it damage how you are raising your child, but it will tear your relationship with your relative apart. It really will.

NANNY OR NANNY SHARE

If you can afford it, nothing beats the one-on-one home care a nanny gives. Nannies are trained or experienced in giving infants 100 percent of what they need, including stimulating activities, as well as taking care of the needs of any other children. Nanny deals with everything. She's there when your baby is sick, to take her to the doctor, to make organic baby food. In other words, to meet the needs of your baby's emotional, mental, and social well-being. She's been police checked and knows CPR. And if you get along well, she'll do the local dry cleaning run too!

Some people with one child find another family with an infant and share a nanny. Either way, it's crucially important to find a great nanny, and that also means being willing (and able) to pay for it. I always say, "Pay peanuts, get monkeys." Simple as that. I find it amazing how people always judge the wages of a professional nanny. When we walk into Gucci and see a bag, we don't go up to the manager and say, "That bag for six hundred dollars. Can you knock it down two hundred dollars?" Yet a nanny's price is always dinner table talk. Your child is the most precious thing in your life! Don't cut corners. We know our stuff.

There are two ways to find a great nanny: word of mouth and reputable nanny agencies. Most of my work was through word of mouth. Once you get onto the parent network through your prenatal classes, etc., you meet other parents who can refer you. Or you can go the agency route. There are two kinds of nannies: those who are formally trained and have certificates and those who have had a lot of experience and no formal training, like me. If you use an agency, they will be a security check. If not, be sure to check references thoroughly.

When interviewing a nanny, most people hand the baby over to the nanny because they want to see how their child responds to her. But that can be, to be honest with you, quite tricky. Because the baby just might grouchy that day and coincidentally start to cry when the nanny's holding him. Of course you need to pay attention to how she is with children, but it's important that you feel good about her too. You need a nanny that you can have a relationship with. Have more than one interview to know that the two of you can gel. This person's coming into your life and spending twelve hours a day or more with your child. She has to be the right person.

Here are some important interview questions:

- What's her experience with newborns?
- What's her opinion on nutrition? Does she cook? You don't need her to be Nigella Lawson, but an ability to put a decent meal on the table is great.
- Is she social and outgoing? Is she somebody who's going to connect with other nannies and moms so that your baby will meet other children?
- Is she flexible and able to work around circumstances while maintaining a healthy routine?
- Does she have maturity, energy, and a good positive mind-set?
- Is she punctual?
- Is she loving and positive? Does she have empathy?
- Will she go on vacation with you if you would like her to?
- Do you share the same beliefs and attitudes about child rearing? Do you think you will be able to learn from one another to sustain a wonderful working relationship?
- How long does she want to work for you, and how long do you want her for?
- What, if any, is her religion and how does that play into yours and her work as a nanny?
- If this is a nanny share, do you think she will be able to give both infants what they need? Is she trained in caring for more than one infant?

Ultimately you're looking for somebody you can welcome as part of your family because this is an incredibly intimate situation. I've had amazing relationships with the families that I've worked with and keep in contact with them even now, seventeen years on. Trust your gut. If you feel you need a nanny camera to validate the choice that you've made, then you've not made the right choice. We've all seen terrible things on the TV and heard of such things. If you don't feel sure, bring that woman back in and ask her any question you want. Because at the end of the day, it's your child. If she's not right, then she hasn't got the job.

You can really make up the rules. Are you going to have her on two-month trial? Is she going to go on vacations with you? What about confidentiality? Try to get all the issues on the table in advance. Write up a contract with the needs of the child and what you expect so there are no surprises down the line.

DAY CARE CENTER

If you're considering this option, look at every day care center within your home or work vicinity. Check out exactly what the staff-child ratio is. Make sure they're licensed so that all the safety issues are taken care of. Are things nice and clean? Hygiene is critical for babies. Is it a happy, colorful environment? You don't want a sober, gray center. Do the other children seem happy? You want to feel good about taking your child there and know that your child's going to be happy there. Get references from other parents.

There will be a routine, no doubt, which you can see. Find out the basics:

- Is the place hygienic?
- Do you provide food or do they?
- What are the ages of the children?
- What activities do they do?
- What educational toys are available?
- Does each baby get individual attention?
- Is there interaction with older children? I think that's perfectly fine as long as the needs of the younger ones are met and there is a separation as to who does what so your newborn's needs are being met regardless.

- What's the educational philosophy of the director? Does there seem to be good communication among people who work there? How will they communicate with you about what's happened with your baby that day?

In the end, it's like when you walk into a house that feels great: you want to have that feeling when you walk into a day care center. And I would recommend always visiting not just on open-house day but also unexpectedly so you can see it in motion when they're not expecting visitors.

Take into account that with day care, if one baby gets a cold, they all get it. Your baby is going to be sicker than other infants because of exposure to all those germs. And generally, you cannot bring a sick baby to day care, so you're going to have to come home from work to care for him. New parents often don't expect that, but it is a reality of institutional care.

CHILD MINDER

Another option is a child minder who, alone or with an assistant, cares for a few babies and/or toddlers in their home. I have no problem with that, as long as you make sure she is licensed. Licensing ensures that she has the proper safety precautions, educational toys, child–adult ratios, etc. In other words, that she and her house are equipped to provide for the safety and the needs of the children she has. Ask to see the license.

As with a day care center, ask:

- Exactly what do you do with the children all day? Is there a timetable/routine?
- Can I have a diary of what my baby does each day to track her progress?
- Do I provide food or do you? Ask for a weekly sheet of what she feeds your baby if you don't have to bring food in.
- Do you provide diapers?
- Are you open during holidays or will I need to find alternative help? What is your sick policy?

- How many children do you look after during the day? At what times? What ages are they? What does the law say about that? How many kids are you authorized to have? She should know the laws and be able to tell you them.
- What are your experience and training, and the experience and training of your assistants?

Make sure you also notice what she's like as a person. Character is important, as with a nanny. A good relationship between the two of you is key. It's your prerogative as a parent to make sure you will feel satisfied in leaving your child. Peace of mind goes a long, long, long, long way.

CHAPTER 3

Essential Equipment for Provisioning Your Baby

hen you begin to get ready to have a baby or read in magazines how much it's going to cost, you may be thinking, "I can't afford a baby." Or, "Oh my word! Where are we going to find that amount of money?" No one ever said raising a child is cheap, especially the first year, because you need a lot of special equipment that is particularly pricey.

Don't get put off. As I always tell my families, people have been having babies for centuries and you'll figure it out. That's why hand-me-downs and baby showers are so wonderful!

Despite being tempted by all kinds of cute items—and I encourage the fun of getting wrapped up in a little fluff—be practical. Your baby doesn't need that size 0–3 month adorable winter coat if she's born in the summer. Remember, babies grow very quickly! You never need as much as you think you will. After all, how many sweaters can one infant use, unless you've got a refluxy baby, in which case you may go through quite a few. That's why parents end up buying so much. They think, "We'd better get this, just in case!" Just in case of what? These days, we're definitely the "just in case" parents—all but the kitchen sink.

Be realistic. Do you really need a bottle warmer? Know what you've got in your purse and know want you need. If you're a parent who can afford it and you want it even if you don't need it, I'm fine with that. After all, it's your choice. If you decide that you want to buy the bottle warmer because you want the lot, then do it! Just know that a few months from now, you're going to be reselling it because you've realized that some of these things are more trouble than they're worth. As in, "I can't faff around at two o'clock in the morning with this bottle warmer."

To help you know what's realistic, I've included in this chapter the must-have essentials that I've learned through experience will ensure your baby's comfort and safety.

One key thing to know that affects all bedding and clothing choices is that babies can't regulate their temperature very well until they are about six months old. So it's easy for them to get overheated or too cold. It's up to you to keep the temperature right through layering of clothes and blankets. So when considering the basic layette, think about when your baby will be born, because that will affect the kind and quantity of your choices.

When it comes to the big-ticket items like car seats, strollers, high chairs, and cribs, I believe in buying the best quality and making sure you can afford it. As opposed to buying the best you can afford. That might mean saving money during your pregnancy to be able to afford the best. Whenever you can get hypoallergenic materials—mattress, sheets, etc.—go for it. As an allergy sufferer, I am a big fan of hypoallergenic. It's natural and breathable.

I advise having the nursery set up, with supplies in place and a packet of burp cloths and clothes already washed in hot water and ready to go, three to four weeks before your due date. That way, even if your baby is early, you're prepared. Being ready in advance will give you a measure of reassurance, so that you're not panicking just before. It's so much easier to come home from the hospital when you've got everything you need on hand. Don't open all the packages of newborn clothes, however, until after the baby is born. That way you can return them if they are too small or too large.

ESSENTIAL EQUIPMENT

Don't be afraid to borrow things or buy them used, with one big exception: *never* use a hand-me-down car seat. This you *must* purchase new because of safety concerns. If you get a hand-me-down crib, be sure it meets current safety standards, and be sure to purchase a new mattress because mattresses are made with special air pockets at the front for the safety of the baby and you want one that's not worn down.

When considering other hand-me-down or secondhand items, be sure to check for durability, cleanliness, and wear and tear. You want to make sure the safety features still work. Is the Velcro on the baby sling still sticky? Does the seat belt on the stroller work? Are the handles on the bassinet beginning to fray? That's potentially dangerous because they could break when you're carrying your baby. Are the slats on the crib close enough together so the baby can't put her head through? Make sure you know what the current safety standards are and that the used equipment matches them.

BASSINET

These are practical for keeping baby cuddled up and close by you wherever you go as well as for sleeping in during the first few months. Be sure the bottom is sturdy enough to support your baby's weight. I recommend using the basket instead of a crib until your baby can turn over or there is no longer room for him to stretch. Newborns have just come from a compact space, so they like to feel snug but not cramped.

You can buy a stand to put the basket on in the bedroom or place it on the floor to Mom's side, or at the foot of the bed if away from home. I prefer using the stand, but either way is fine, as long as you can't step on it or knock it over. Make sure the basket locks into the stand so it can't fall. During the day, when you move it around with you, be sure to place it on the floor, not a table or chair.

They're usually sold with a one-inch vinyl mattress and sheet. Some come with bumpers, but I suggest removing them—there's not much room to begin with, the basket is soft enough that it won't cause bumps, and there's nowhere to tie the bumpers.

CRIB

When your baby outgrows the bassinet, it's time for a crib. Be sure you buy one that meets current safety standards. Practice dropping the sides to test if they're quiet and easy for you to maneuver. Make sure the mattress fits snugly against the sides so that baby can't wriggle or get wedged under, and make sure the bumper pads fit snugly to the sides and are attached with short ties always tied on the outside not inside to prevent smothering and strangulation. When installed properly, bumpers are good in cribs because they prevent babies' legs from getting caught in the slats. Some parents buy two bumper pads to go all the way around.

BABY SLING

I swear by a sling. It allows you to be mobile and keep the baby physically connected to you. It also allows Dad to have physical closeness. Make sure it provides proper neck and head support, is made of a washable fabric, feels comfortable on you, has strong safety tabs so it can't come undone, and permits you to carry your baby facing out or in. In the beginning, you'll want to have her facing in. As she gets older, she'll want to face out and experience the world.

There is an array of fashionable slings around these days. I say, try them all and you decide. When figuring out which to buy, make sure you take into consideration your width. It's kind of like driving a car and going through barriers. You have a sense of how wide your car is so you can tell if you can fit. You've got to know how much space you plus baby in sling will take! It's like being very pregnant—you have to take into account you're sticking out more in front or to the side.

CHANGING MAT

This is a plastic pad that you put down in order to change your baby. You can put a towel on top of it so your baby won't feel cold plastic. These mats are great because they allow you to change your baby anywhere—on a clean floor, a bed, a table.

If you have the budget, you can also purchase a fancy changing table, but I don't recommend them as a necessity because they're expensive and babies can fall off them very easily. Plus the amount of time you can use them is short.

But I bet you have one, right? You went into the baby store and saw the crib. And the matching set of drawers. And the matching mahogany changing table. And you thought, "Oh, let's buy all three to go nicely." I'm convinced it's the one piece that in the end, you always say, "What a waste of money!" Because babies start wiggling, you realize the drawers are too small to be of any use, and you give up on it by the time she hits eight months.

If you do buy a changing table, make sure you use the safety strap. And if you're changing him any place that's off the ground, be sure everything you need is within reach so you don't have to let go of him, even for a second. If anything, it will take the strain off your back, and that's worth something!

CHEST OF DRAWERS

Some changing tables include drawers for clothes, which are always too small, I've found. I suggest instead that you buy something that your child can use to store clothes for years to come. Make sure it's heavy so it can't be pulled over by adventurous toddlers.

STROLLER

Before your baby can sit up well, around six months, she must be in a stroller that allows her to lie down flat. Once she can sit up, you can have her upright in a stroller. Most good strollers have the capacity to convert from flat to upright. In choosing one, also consider durability, sturdiness, and ease of use. How easy is it to fold? To carry up and down stairs if you must do that? To put the brakes on? It shouldn't have to be rocket science to take your baby for a walk.

I like to think of a stroller as a shell for your baby. You want a shell that is comfortable and has enough space for your little one to lie down in. Check the wheels. Some strollers only roll well on pavement and have trouble on gravel. You want one that is mobile wherever you go.

BABY MONITOR

These gadgets are godsends, allowing you to know what's happening when you're in another room, say, taking a shower. Go for the mobile kind that can strap to your belt, like the pace steppers that show you how many steps you've taken.

Consider a rechargeable. It's more expensive up front, but will save money on batteries. Make sure it has a low-battery indicator as well as an indicator when you've gone out of range. You can buy one that not only monitors sound, but movement and even the temperature of a room.

With modern technology, some parents are tempted to buy TV monitors. I wouldn't say not to, but if you do, use it to help you learn to distinguish the noises your child makes when she's crying: when she's really unhappy, when she's petering out, when she makes sounds in her sleep. You want to become intuitively in tune with your baby. In the past, parents had to use their instincts to learn their baby's cries. This gadget can make it easier. Be aware though, that if you thought you were a couch potato before, now you'll certainly one—sitting there staring at the screen of your little one all night long.

BABY BATHTUB

I love the new small plastic baths that fit over the bathtub. When you're done, you pull the plug and the water all comes out into the main bath. They're easy on your back. After giving birth, your back muscles may be a little bit weak, and these tubs mean you don't have to lean over so far. But if you can't afford one, you can always use a plastic basin and put it on the floor. The new blow-up baths are also great—practical and easy to travel with.

The reason why it's important to start off with a small bath is because in a small space with just a little water, you'll gain confidence in how to hold and handle her. If you lose your grip, you're not losing it to the capacity and hardness of a big bath.

And of course you never leave her unattended even for a second, no matter what bath arrangement you choose.

HIGH CHAIR

You won't need this until your baby is around six months, so you might want to put off this purchase until then as a way of spreading out your expenses. When you do buy one, be sure it has a way to strap your baby in and use it! Consider how easy it is to clean and store. Leather and hard plastic ones are good to clean.

CAR SEAT AND SAFETY SEAT

Your baby *must always* be in a car seat whenever you drive anywhere. No penny-pinching on the car seat and remember, no used seats. All new car seats must conform to the U.S. government's most stringent safety standards so when you buy it new, you ensure you're getting the safest.

Until one year of age and at least twenty pounds, babies must ride rear facing in the rear seat and at a 30–45-degree angle to keep their heads from falling forward. Car seats for newborns come with inserts to support the head and the neck.

Don't think, "Oh, he'll grow into it." Or, "We'll save a little bit more money." Buy the age- and weight-appropriate one. Period. When you need a new one, you need a new one. When installing, do not tip back too far or he can come out in an accident. Be sure to follow manufacturers' instructions, as well as your car's manual for proper installation.

When shopping for a seat, be sure to test the buckle and imagine putting a fidgeting baby into it. There are a variety of fastening arrangements. Buy the kind that works best for you, but is not so easy that a child can tamper with it.

You can either get a car seat that is able to be used as a carry seat inside the house, or buy a separate seat for that purpose. Either way, recognize that your kid's just been sitting in a seat, say, for a half-hour journey, and he's going to be sitting in there again for however long you take him into the restaurant. So make sure you allow him to get out of the seat indoors as much as possible so he's not constantly sitting in the same bucket position.

OTHER EQUIPMENT TO CONSIDER

Large comfortable rocking chair: Do you want to buy a rocking chair so that you can feed and burp and then place the baby into a basket or bassinet? Some parents (and babies) love them; others don't. To me, it's a matter of personal preference.

Bouncy Seat and/or Swing: I like these because they give your baby something to do that's different. Babies tend to love the motion these provide.

They're also great for when your baby is older as you play alongside her. Don't overuse as a babysitter though.

Playpen: Some people swear by them, others hate them. I believe in using them for play only, not for hours at a time as a babysitter or a way to confine your active baby. Overuse is neglect!

LINENS

I recommend all cotton whether it's toweling or not. It's soft and can be washed in hot water to sterilize.

- Three stretch cotton-fitted sheets for the bassinet, and later, for the crib
- Four flat cotton-top sheets
- Four cotton blankets with waffle weave that can be used for swaddling, putting the baby down on the floor during the day and for sleeping, plus a warmer blanket for winter nights
- Lots of burp cloths (usually cotton diapers) for wiping up messes of all sorts. One was attached to me for seventeen years, like Long John Silver's parrot.
- One set of baby washcloths and towel with hood

CLOTHING

When it comes to babies, winter or summer, it's all about layers. As much as possible, go for all cotton, or at least 80 percent cotton, as this will allow the skin to breathe and prevent the baby from overheating.

Think about practicality and ease of dressing. Does it have snaps or buttons? Buttoning a squirming baby can be very difficult. And do you plan to iron those little dresses? A lot of parents put their babies in jersey-type fleece material because it can just be thrown into the tumble dryer without having to be ironed. Also velour and cotton onesies wash up well time and time again and can be put into the tumble dryer and dried very quickly to use again.

Make sure the crotch opens easily for diaper changing. Avoid clothing that is tight around the neck, arms or legs, or has ties or cords that can suffocate or en-tangle toes and fingers. (Ditto for booties.)

When buying clothes, go light on the 0–3 months sizes until you have your baby. Be aware that white will get stains that may not be bleachable. But it does look beautiful, as you can see from the photos of the babies in this book.

Here's my recommended list:

- 8–10 undershirts; I prefer the ones with snaps to ties
- 3–4 bibs
- 4–6 sleepers
- 4–5 pairs of socks or booties
- 5–7 day outfits like onesies
- 2 sweaters, 3 if it's a winter baby
- 3 cotton caps
- 1 hat with a brim all the way around for when your baby is three months and older
- snowsuit and mittens if it's a winter baby; the fleece ones are particu-larly good
- 3–4 dozen newborn diapers—make sure to keep a supply handy

LAUNDRY BASICS

- Everything should be washed before coming in contact with your baby.
- Babies have sensitive skin, so you should always use a mild detergent that is made especially for babies.
- Wash baby clothes separately from other laundry for the first six months.
- Always use the hot water cycle with bedding, cloth diapers, and bibs to kill bacteria and dust mites that can cause allergies. Be sure to wash bedding at least once a week.
- Don't overfill washer, so that laundry can get properly rinsed.

DIAPERS

Guess how many diapers your bundle of joy is going to go through before he's potty trained? Roughly five thousand! That's a lot of poopy pants. You've basically got four choices:

- Disposables
- Reusable recycled cotton diapers—cotton diapers with disposable liners
- Cloth diapers that you wash yourself
- A diaper service

NANNY'S NO-NO'S

- Pillows: can cause suffocation.
- Duvets or quilts: can cause suffocation or overheating.
- Super-fluffy blankets: fluff can get in nose and mouth and cause breathing difficulties.
- Overloading bassinet or crib with stuffed animals: can collect dust that causes allergies and may be choking or suffocation hazard.
- Talcum powder: particles can injure lungs. I know parents still use it, but please know the facts.
- Dirty diapers in baby's reach: they're germy and not to be touched. Place in closed diaper pail.

The reusable recycled ones are best for the environment. However, the disposable ones are more convenient. The cloth ones take more work, but may be better at preventing diaper rash. You decide based on what matters to you. Is it about convenience? Money? The environment? I believe this is a choice you as a parent should make based on your opinion.

Make sure you also have a good supply of diaper sacks, those fragrant orange-smelling sacks to put dirty diapers in when you are out.

DIAPER BAG

Be prepared to go places with your infant. Get a nice durable bag with large pockets. There are lots of styles out there—choose one that suits the both of you. Mom may find it appealing to walk around in the latest, but Dad might not be very amused. Maybe buy a separate bag for each of you.

Make sure it always has:

waterproof changing pad

- waterproof changing pad
- one change of clothing from head to toe
- 3–4 diapers
- diaper wipes
- cloth diapers for cleaning up spills, faces, etc.
- diaper rash cream
- diaper sacks for dirty diapers
- antibacterial gel to clean your hands
- spare pacifier
- cotton wool
- toys: couple of soft rattles, etc.
- 1 bottle of water for wetting cotton wool, washing, or making a bottle
- plastic spoon

Give it a quick check over each time you go out. Be realistic about where you're going and how long you're going for as well, because you may be out for longer than a couple hours and then realize, "Oh, I've run out of diapers."

As your baby gets older, the things that you place in there will change. You'll go from velour rattles to cardboard books. Add a milk bottle or snack.

OTHER ESSENTIALS

When someone is about to have a baby, I like to make a basket of goodies with the little things that I know parents of a newborn will need. It's meant to be carried from room to room as you need it. You can make one for yourself. Buy a basket, line it with a cloth, and put in the following:

- baby thermometer: for best accuracy, get a digital rectal thermometer. The digital under the arm can't be used on infants under three months and it is less accurate anyway.
- petroleum jelly for rectal thermometer
- olive oil for cradle cap
- diaper rash cream
- unscented baby soap and shampoo
- baby scissors for cutting fingernails and toenails
- a soft baby hairbrush
- baby massage cream

IF BREAST-FEEDING

Here's the equipment you're going to need:

- 2–4 nursing bras: make sure these have wide straps to support your breasts and don't press too tightly against your nipples
- One box of disposable breast pads (so you can experiment with finding the brand you like). Otherwise, you'll be walking around with your breasts leaking all over the place.
- Electric breast pump to express milk to store when milk supply is low, and so Dad or others can also feed the baby to give Mom rest or a chance for rest. You can also try the hand pump, although most women find this challenging.
- A nursing pillow, commonly called a support or *V*-shaped pillow. These are fabulous because they wrap around your body and really support you and the baby as she feeds.

IF BOTTLE-FEEDING OR PUMPING

- 6–8 bent-neck bottles with the soft nipples that flatten at the top like a nipple does
- bottle brush to get all the gunk out
- sterilizer: you can buy an electric one or one to put in the microwave

BABYPROOFING

Babyproofing—making your home safe for your precious infant—really begins before your baby is born with the choices you make about equipment and environment. Here's why: when babies are very young, some of the greatest dangers they face have to do with breathing. To avoid suffocation and strangulation, I've made recommendations about bedding and clothing. But making your home safe for your baby's breathing goes beyond that.

Because their lungs are so tiny, babies breathe many more times a minute than adults. Which means they breathe in more pollutants such as paint fumes, aerosol sprays, tobacco smoke, dust, fibers, etc. that can cause inflammation and asthma. For instance, if a toxic chemical is in the air, a baby will receive twice as much exposure than an adult. So the cleaner and more nontoxic you can keep the environment, the healthier your little one's precious lungs will be.

However, this is going to raise some hard choices for you as parents to make in terms of money and effort before the baby comes along. I've placed these suggestions here purely for you to discuss so that you can make informed choices. Whatever you do, plan to be done 4–6 weeks before the baby's born so things can air out properly:

- If you can afford it, consider using water-based paint in the baby's room that is low in VOCs (volatile organic compounds, like formaldehyde, which are given off as gases). The Internet is a source for a wide range of ecofriendly paints, though you will pay a little more per gallon. Some are 100 percent biodegradable and can be disposed of on a compost heap!
- If you have an older home (built before the seventies) that might have lead paint, have it checked by professionals. Dust from lead paint is extremely toxic, especially to babies' brains.
- Paint two weeks before putting any decorations, furniture, carpet, etc. in the room so that the fumes will dissipate rather than being absorbed.
- If you use wallpaper, you may want to choose one with a nontoxic finish and use nontoxic wallpaper glue. Make sure it has an antifungal in it to stop fungus from growing behind the paper.

- If you want window treatments, consider natural, washable fabrics and wash frequently. Make sure they have no cords or tassels, to avoid strangulation, or buy "breakaway tassels" that will separate if your baby gets tangled. Never place the crib or other furniture near blinds.
- Avoid particleboard furniture (it gives off formaldehyde) or seal it with low VOC sealer.
- Hardwood is better than carpet because carpet can collect dust. However, carpet is more cushy and warm. If you do use carpet, make sure it is tightly woven so that your baby can't pull at it and choke on carpet fluff. Make sure you air it out for at least three days after it's installed before you put your baby in the room, and make sure you vacuum at least once a week to keep down dust, mites, and other pollutants.
- Consider using nontoxic cleaners rather than aerosol sprays such as furniture polish or air fresheners. For all kinds of healthy products, check out www.ecomall.com.
- Install smoke detectors and carbon monoxide detectors on every floor of your house (and have a carbon monoxide detector by your furnace as well).
- Consider getting a cold air humidifier. It gets rid of dry air, and helps especially when babies have colds, flu, or stuffy noses from living in centrally heated housing.

PART II

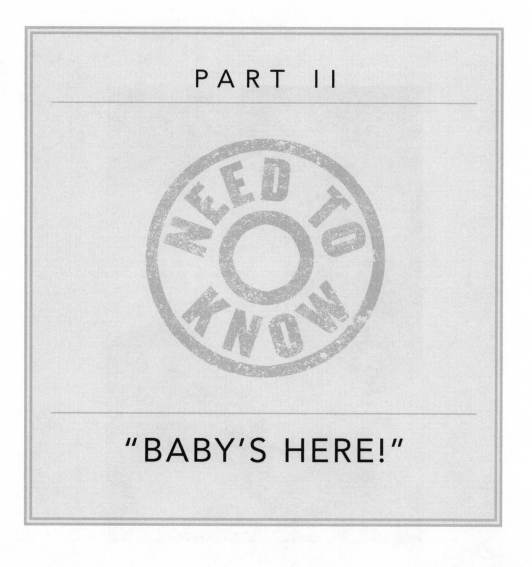

"BABY'S HERE!"

CHAPTER 4

Zero to Three Months

 PARENTS' JOURNEY

This section is about helping you eliminate as much as possible those worries about yourself as a parent so you can enjoy the process. I'm here to lend support for what you're feeling and thinking, and to reassure you that the things that are difficult will pass and to experience the joy as much as possible. Here's my key message: your love is enough. In fact, it's just what your baby needs!

Just as your baby grows and changes a lot this year, so will you. Your baby will bring out qualities you never had before, and will challenge you to develop even more patience, maturity, and humor. You'll be surprised at how your emotional development goes in similar stages as your child: the first three months, 3–6, 6–9, and 9–12. By the time a year rolls around, you'll be an old hand but a warm one!

0–3 Months

Your baby is finally here! It might be everything you thought it would be, or nothing like it at all. Because the reality of parenthood is different from any ideas about it, you may be surprised or even shocked by the intensity of your feelings. You may find yourself sobbing from the intense experience of being a parent, astonished at how strong your feelings of love are. Or you can feel an overpowering sense of responsibility that this tiny creature is completely dependent on you. Or you may feel anxious: Is my baby okay? Am I doing it right? Or any of a wide array of emotions. Parents who've already had a child may be surprised by the difference in their emotions this time around. There's no predicting exactly how you will feel.

At first it can seem rather overwhelming. Here's this little being who's exercising his lungs like an opera singer, who's totally relying on you for his every need and want. And he can't even tell you verbally what those needs are, although he is communicating through his cry. You're on constantly and working out how you're going to fit everything in: Do I do the laundry now or after I clean those bottles? When am I supposed to take a shower? How do I do everything else and deal with my little one?

That dependency takes getting used to. I've had experiences looking after newborns when a parent's said to me, "I'm just going off to the shop with the baby to get some food for the weekend." And they've walked out and forgot to take the baby! Because they're so used to living with only having to worry about themselves. I must say we both found the humor in this.

On top of everything else you're feeling—as if it's not enough—you may experience an overpowering sense of disbelief that you've actually just given birth to this little baby who's lying next to you. What's really lovely is the language that I see between two parents when they don't say anything, just look at each other in amazement at the miracle they've created. You're probably taking photos 24-7 and your baby's entered the world of the paparazzi. Those baby albums do make me laugh—parents take *hundreds* of pictures of their baby at first, and now with all the new technology, there are loads of baby movies and Web sites too.

Some parents find this stage difficult because there's no interaction from a newborn. Their presence is the interaction. Just them being there—a live present. And she's a miracle that changes, day to day, week to week. Soon there will be interaction aplenty.

Try not to get too upset if you don't do all the parenting tasks up to scratch. Baby care takes a while to get the hang of. There may be *Exorcist* moments when milk comes back out. Or the poo goes flying. I remember flying poo with new dads. They didn't realize that the poo shot out! There they are thinking to themselves, "How come this baby didn't come with an apron?" These moments will make for priceless stories when they're older. Look for the humor, because there will definitely be moments when it's either laugh or cry, hormones and all.

Anytime the baby is asleep, you may find yourself checking constantly to make sure she's okay. Then you double-check yourself to make sure that it's okay to be checking if the baby's okay, to make sure that *you're* okay. Generally this is very normal. Because this is your baby! There's a very fine line, though, when you create more anxiety for yourself than necessary. But that often has a lot to do with hormones as well as experience, and will even out over time. If you are worried about yourself just a little, talk to your doctor. It will not hurt.

Bonding

One common worry is about bonding. Parents think that they should *instantly* feel overwhelming connectedness to their baby. And some people do feel that. But for others, these feelings grow over time as you come to know him and care for him. So don't worry too much about how you're reacting, as long as you're not experiencing the intense darkness and real negativity of postnatal depression. (More on that a bit later).

Hopefully you've got at least one extra pair of hands to fetch and carry so that you can focus on giving your baby lots of love and attention. It's important to understand that there's no such thing as spoiling a baby! The more you comfort, coddle, cuddle, and care for him, particularly in these early months and over this first year, the less needy and whiny he's likely to be when he's a toddler and child. Babies are totally, completely dependent. So when we meet their needs swiftly and accurately, we give them the sense of security they need to become independent, confident children.

There comes a period of time where you realize, "Oh, I just spent two hours staring at my baby!" That's good. That's what you're supposed to be doing. In the beginning, it's all about putting in time, just watching your baby and bonding. You can only connect if you spend time. That's how you get to know him, to see his body language, his little facial expressions. You think that she's given you that first smile until you realize she's just passed gas.

So make sure during that first month that there are lots of loose corners just to lie around and bond with your baby. Be realistic in your expectations of everything else. Don't get too hung up about the state of the house. Of course there needs to be cleanliness. But there's no need to be germaphobic. This doesn't mean that you don't have to take into account your other children if you have them and the realities of daily life. But this is a once-in-a-lifetime experience, and the time goes so quickly. So relish, relish.

Mom's Body Changes

The first weeks after you give birth, your body will be readjusting. Your uterus will shrink, you'll bleed heavily vaginally as your uterus sheds its lining, your volume of blood will reduce, your hormones will fluctuate, your belly will be less firm, and your breasts will prepare to breast-feed. Your perinea may be sore and you may experience constipation. You may feel faint or dizzy, and find yourself shivering and/or sweating a lot. Oh, and that thick pregnancy hair may fall out. Some women take this time as a new beginning and get their hair cut as a rite of passage to motherhood. If you find your breasts have changed, use support push-up bras and go for a fitting to leave you feeling all woman again after breast-feeding.

Some women develop infections of the reproductive tract. Symptoms include:

- abdominal pain
- fever
- vaginal discharge
- difficulty urinating

See your doctor if you're experiencing any of these.

Despite what you may think from the tabloids, don't expect to return to your pre-pregnancy weight overnight. Women fall prey to impossible standards due to media coverage of famous new mothers who have personal trainers and tummy tucks, etc. How quickly you'll bounce back depends on your body and your age. It's not impossible, with exercise and a good healthy food plan. There's no reason you can't look the way you want to.

Because you burn a lot of calories when you breast-feed, I have seen women breast-feed constantly, not because their baby needs it, but because it helps them lose weight. This is dangerous because the baby is getting more than he needs, and breast-feeding is being used for the wrong reason. Be sensible and do what's right for your child and yourself!

Recovery from a Cesarean

If you've had a C-section, you will need even more downtime. You may experience greater fatigue, soreness around the incision, discomfort upon urinating, and gas pains in your guts, shoulders, and upper chest. Here are some tips for a speedy recovery:

- Keep your incision area clean and dry and expose it to air.
- Be sure you get as much lying around on the sofa time as possible for the first couple weeks. Avoid a lot of stair-climbing if you can.
- No exercising for at least six weeks.
- No driving.
- When sneezing, coughing, or laughing, hold a pillow against your incision to reduce pain.
- No heavy lifting until the incision has healed.
- Rocking and moving around can help eliminate gas pains.
- Breast-feed so that your baby's legs are under your arms.

The Baby Blues and Postnatal Depression

For most women, the hormonal and emotional changes from giving birth combined with fatigue and the newness of the experience cause what's known as the baby blues. Signs include:

- irritability
- sadness
- anxiety or fear
- anger

You may experience any or all of these emotions. The blues typically come on a few days after giving birth and last for a few days, tapering off as your hormones level off and you get into a rhythm with your baby.

Lots of mothers get thrown because they have an idea of how they should be feeling, which runs counter to what is actually happening to them emotionally and chemically. You may find your mind telling you one thing while your body's screaming, "No!" Understand that your hormones will straighten them-selves out and try to let go of expecting things to be a certain way so that you can enjoy them as they are as much as possible.

Dads can get their own version of the baby blues. They may suddenly start to worry about their ability to provide for the family. They may feel conflicted about taking on such a huge responsibility. These worries are natural. The more you get in there and share the experience with your partner, the more comfort-able with your role you're going to be.

Some women, about one in ten, have a more intense experience known as postnatal, or postpartum, depression, which can last up to a year. It is a mental and emotional illness. Here are the signs:

- extreme sadness, emptiness, and despair
- severe feelings of inadequacy
- withdrawal from friends and family
- an inability to care for their children
- dark thoughts of harming their baby or themselves
- panic attacks, feelings of anxiety
- lethargy
- chest pains, abdominal pains, or breathing problems that have no med-ical explanation
- drinking too much, abuse of prescription drugs
- obsessive or repetitive behavior
- putting on a brave face

If you are experiencing any of these symptoms, please see your doctor. This condition can be successfully treated with antidepressant medicine. You may also want to get counseling or other mental and physical support.

It also helps to become more consciously aware of how you're feeling. Are you worried your baby is going to catch germs? Are you anxious over your ability to mother well? Really analyze where the feelings are coming from. Then ask for support from somebody who's close to you. When you bring your fears out into the open in the presence of someone who really cares about you, it helps.

If someone who is close to you suggests that you might have postnatal depression, please take them seriously. And dads, if you suspect postnatal depression in your partner, help her get help. I know relatives who were aware of what was going on but were afraid to say something.

If you do have depression, try not to beat yourself up. I'm concerned that women with postnatal depression label themselves as failures as moms from the beginning. This is how I see it: some women get it, just like some babies get jaundice. It's not a failure on your part.

Do positive things to support yourself during this time. Yoga, Pilates, meditation, and swimming are things that allow us to focus on ourselves for a bit.

Nurturing Yourself

The first three months are all about giving your baby what she needs in order to continue to develop from just coming out of the womb. You know she needs sleep, so you create an environment that supports her to be able to peacefully sleep the amount of time she requires. And you support yourself if you're breast-feeding by eating and sleeping well so that she will have the nourishment she needs.

Because your baby won't always sleep for long periods of time, you won't either. Sleep deprivation means you may find yourself laughing and crying at the same time because you're exhausted. And what used to matter in terms of housework or watching TV or talking or sex doesn't matter as much anymore because your priority is sleep. That's why I say if the baby's sleeping, you should be too, especially during the first month.

I'm a strong believer that mothers of newborns need nurturing as much as infants do. To nurture, you need nurturing. It helps you to have the ability to deal with crying and all the needs your baby has. This can be difficult because even though you've cut the physical umbilical cord there's an invisible one too. Don't worry, it will be there no matter where you go!

Nurturing is about allowing yourself good things to eat, a relaxing environment, enjoyable creature comforts, taking an hour off to nap. How are you taking care of yourself physically? Mentally, what are you doing to keep yourself stimulated? This is a time to spoil yourself and to let others spoil you. In the past, new mothers were surrounded by a whole group of women who nurtured them. If you're lucky enough to have that, enjoy.

But because so many of us no longer have that kind of support, we have to give it to ourselves. The key question is, "What is it that nurtures me? What makes me go, 'Ahhhhh.' " A mani/pedi? A massage? A nice soak? A read in bed? Then think about how you can get more of those things right now. This is not being selfish. In order to give your incredible love, care, and nurturing to this other being, you've got to be receiving it yourself too, or else you end up with an empty well. If you can't honor yourself to give that to yourself, then how are you going to be able to give nonstop to your baby?

Many new moms and dads tell me about an animalistic feeling of protection that arises as soon as the baby is born. That you would willingly die for this being. But rather than saying, "I would die for you," how about "I would live for you"? When we think of it that way, we take good care of ourselves because it's the responsible, natural thing to do for us and for our baby.

Dealing with Crying

In the section on Parentcraft, I give tips for soothing your baby. Here I want to talk about how you can deal emotionally with your baby's crying. Tiny infants, especially if they're refluxy, cry a lot. And new parents can feel overwhelmed by that, especially when they're alone. You try everything and he's still wailing. At times you might think to yourself, I just want to make this baby be quiet! You could even feel resentment or anger at your child. No matter how bad it gets, there are certain unacceptable behaviors you must not do:

- shaking the baby
- hitting the baby
- putting a pillow over the baby's mouth to quiet her

So what can you do? One thing is to learn to inhale the cry and send out a sense of calm. It's like when you have a toothache. If you don't get engulfed in it, you can go with the pulse until you don't actually feel the pain. Slow, deep breaths will also help you stay calm.

If that doesn't work, give yourself five minutes. Put her down in her bassinet, go out of the room, and regroup. Just give yourself a chance to calm down, then go back and pick the baby up again. Make sure you go back! Because you don't want her to associate any discomfort with being neglected or forgotten about. You're taking five minutes as a breather, as a pit stop, to be able to calmly pick your child back up again. If after five minutes you still aren't calm, call someone—a friend, a neighbor, or relative.

I hear mothers, especially, feeling guilty if they ever feel annoyed with their baby. They're exhausted and then the baby starts crying and they feel guilty for their feelings. They're not being violent or shaking the baby, but they feel guilty just for feeling frustrated. I think that comes from a good place. You feel guilty because your baby is 100 percent innocence and purity, and you know your thoughts are not of purity. Unless your feelings are impacting the way you behave toward your baby or other people in your life, just acknowledge them and don't beat yourself up over it.

I strongly suggest you join a support group of new parents. Other people's stories create a great sense of reassurance that what you're experiencing is normal to others too. You can find such community from the people in your Lamaze class or through community bulletin boards. Or by meeting people at a music class, or in the park. Go to the places where there are babies. You can also find support online at my Web site (www.jofrost.com). Check out the resource guide for more suggestions. These relationships are also a great source of friends for your child.

Support Check

Now that you have your baby in your arms, it's time to make sure that you've got all the support you need. Your ideas of what you would need and the reality may be very different, particularly if you have a colicky baby. Would a cleaning person help you feel less overwhelmed? Is there someone who could come in a few hours a week so you could nap? Don't be afraid to ask for more help if you need it.

It's particularly important that there's a unity between Mom and Dad in understanding the priority at this time, which in breast-feeding mothers is to make sure she gets enough sleep so she's able to produce milk.

Mom, as I said earlier, this is no time to wear the martyr crown. Give him the chance to care for his own baby, to make mistakes. Because then he'll be there over time as a fifty-fifty parent. Some dads just completely surprise themselves by being naturally great daddies. Others learn "in the field." Either way is fine and normal.

If, Mom, you think to yourself as your back is breaking, "The baby will only go off to sleep if I hold her. Only I know the right way to feed her. . . ." you're your own worst enemy. (Well, someone had to tell you.) Eventually your partner will think, "You're the only one who can do it right? Then go ahead and do it!" Men can get pushed out and then women complain of not having their help. When I meet a mom like that, I say, "Oh, here we go! Spit and polish. Polish up that crown!"

Recognize where that martyr thing is coming from. Usually it's a result of mothers needing their baby to need them. Or believing that, because they were the birth vessel, the mother ship, they somehow "own" this child more than Dad. This is dangerous because their baby is being treated as a possession, rather than a living, breathing human being who needs the love and care of the adults around her. I feel sorry for fathers in those circumstances. So, Mom, check yourself and make sure to accept all available help, particular from your child's father.

WHAT WENT RIGHT TODAY?

As you are learning how to care for your newborn and tracking her sleeping and feeding in the baby log in the back of the book, I feel it's also very important to look at the positive things that have come out of the day. That way you can see that you're doing a lot of things right, which will create a positive attitude that will help you and your baby. All you need to do just before you fall asleep is ask yourself, "What went right today?" It's a wonderful thing to do with your partner too, as a way of sharing successes of parenthood. And remember, even if things went wrong, it's still positive because you now know what to do next time.

Dealing with Older Children

As much as you need to spend time with your newborn, you absolutely need to carve out time to be with your firstborn too, together as a family and separately with each parent. Because otherwise it's like Mommy or Daddy's been taken away to never-never land.

Be sensitive introducing your newborn to your child. Don't leave them alone together. Because your firstborn is going to want to climb into the bassinet and have a good old peek in a loving way. Or try to share food or a toy with the baby. Or "I love you so much, let me give you a *big* hug." It can all be in the nicest of ways (or not). But either way, you have to curb their behavior and teach them to be gentle.

How you respond to these incidents is incredibly important. You need not to be short-tempered but to use your tone, if she's at least eighteen months, to say, "No. We don't touch the baby that way. We do it this way." Then move her aside. You have to be militant in those circumstances because your baby could be in danger. It's not funny when your two-year-old decides she's going to bounce the baby by his feet. You need to teach consideration and awareness. This will take time if the firstborn is young.

Depending on the age of the older child, you may also find that she suddenly sees the baby as something to experiment with: "Hmm, if I do this, the baby will cry. Or I can push the baby off the sofa and watch her fall." She might find this funny. It's important not to take this too seriously, while protecting your infant and instructing your older one as to how to behave. It does not mean he hates his sister, just that he needs to learn how to treat her. Show the older one how to behave as well as give consequences for bad behavior. It is okay to facially show you're not happy with their actions, or upset.

Some days or weeks after the birth, the realization kicks in for the older child that the baby's not returnable. Then you may have questions like "When is this baby leaving?" Try not to think, "She hates the baby!" Your firstborn is just trying to figure out where she fits into this new world. Does she still matter? It's your job to make her realize that of course, she's still here and she's a very big part of the family, and that the birth of the new one doesn't threaten that.

Your words of reassurance, your attention, will make all the difference. You may get negative words or behaviors from her, but these tend to be short-lived if you respond with positivity and attention. The actual moments of negativity by older children are usually very short, even if at the time it feels serious.

The most common response I find with older children around their new sibling is that they remember that rattle or crib as theirs and get possessive about such things: "That's mine!" You can't dispute the fact that it was. So instead say, "Yes, it was yours, and we're giving it to the baby now because it's a *baby* toy and you're a big girl now."

I also don't like talk such as, "We can't do this because of the baby. We can't do that because of the baby." Because then the older child gets the idea that the baby is a burden, because she's stopping him from doing the things he wants. Instead, figure out whether you can or you can't do something and then state, for instance, "We have to feed the baby first because when you're a baby you have to eat very often. Then we can do what you want." That way you're teaching your child about babies, as well as how to take turns and share attention.

Don't expect your firstborn to suddenly know how to do things just because you wish he could. I see this a lot. The firstborn has been babied and cared for and suddenly, when a newborn arrives, parents assume that the older will magically know how to tie his shoes, or get his dinner from the fridge and cook it. The poor firstborn is sitting there thinking, you've always done everything for me. I don't know how to put the buckle through the Velcro and now you haven't got time to show me how to do it.

This gets misconstrued by children as your not caring. So make sure you continue to help the firstborn so that he doesn't feel abandoned. Don't just expect him to know things you haven't taught him. Otherwise you may notice him regressing in his development for your attention. Because he's figured it out that it's cool to be a baby because babies get attention. This is where you ask the gods for patience, patience, and more patience!

DEVELOPMENTAL OVERVIEW

I've include this section in each age stage so that you can get a sense of your baby's growth. It's human nature to want to understand where your baby is in terms of physical, mental, and social growth, and whether that's on target. You're in love with your baby. And you want to understand because you want to be able to do as much as you possibly can for this little one. That's fabulous.

I also want you to understand that most likely what's happening with your baby is natural. Crying, for instance, is the nature of infancy. The more you understand the natural stages, the more you can accept and flow with your baby's development.

Please be aware that each infant is unique and develops at her own pace, so these time frames are not cast in stone. There are tremendous variations in when babies walk, talk, get teeth, sleep through the night, etc. Don't have a heart attack if your baby's two months behind. Don't compare your baby to others. It's a bad habit to start that can be extremely damaging to your child's self-esteem as she gets older. Plus, it causes needless worry on your part.

Rather, use this information as a guide so that it brings awareness for things that might have to be checked out if they are delayed beyond a bit. As the primary carer, you spend more time around your baby than anyone else. And that's why when you go to your baby's doctor, he or she relies on your input to understand how your baby is doing. So the more you have an idea of general development, the more you can mentally log how your baby is doing. And by all means, if you have concerns, talk to your pediatrician.

Successful Doctor Visits

In the first year, babies are seen by the pediatrician for two weeks, then at two-, four-, six-, nine-, and twelve-month checkups. And of course, if you have any concerns between visits, don't hesitate to have your baby seen.

- Buy a baby book to track her progress. It should have places to record height and weight, immunizations, illnesses, etc. The more you keep this up to date, the easier it will be to answer the doctor's questions during checkups or an emergency.
- Ideally both parents should be present to ask questions and to help with dressing and undressing for the first visit. Then work it out between you how best that suits your family dynamics.
- Keep a written list of your concerns and questions so that you won't forget something.

Because newborns change rapidly in the first few weeks, I've divided the developmental overview of the first three months into days.

Physical Development:

1–30 DAYS
In the very beginning, your baby spends most of his time sleeping, eating, and filling those diapers. And of course communicating (otherwise known as crying) if he needs something—food, a dry diaper, comfort, a change of scenery, a blanket

on or off, to be held. There is a tremendous variation in how much newborns cry. If he has colic, it can be for many hours a day. Your baby isn't doing this to annoy or frustrate you. Think of it as your baby talking to you. And while he may spend 14–18 hours a day sleeping, in the beginning he is not able to sleep more than 2–4 hours at a stretch without needing to feed. That's because his stomach is only the size of his fist!

At first, your baby may lose weight—about one-tenth of her birth weight over the first five days, although I've known bigger babies who haven't. Weight loss is normal because babies are born with excess fluid. By about day five, she'll begin to gain so that by day ten, she'll be back to her birth weight. Growth will then go in spurts, with weight gain averaging two-thirds of an ounce per day and growing about 1–1½ inches the first month. Boys tend to gain a bit more weight than girls and be slightly longer. During the first month, your baby's skull will grow faster than at any other point in her life, about 1 inch in circumference.

Any swelling of her eyelids or bruising during delivery will disappear, as will the fine hair that may have covered her head. So will her blotchy skin, which may appear blue or pink. Around week three, the umbilical cord stump should fall off. It may still have a raw patch that you need to keep clean and dry, which should disappear by week five.

By week four or so, you may notice baby acne appearing. It's a normal condition due to hormones that crossed the placenta during birth. It's often made worse by her lying in sheets laundered in harsh detergents or spit-up milk. Here's how I minimize the problem: place a cloth diaper under her head when she's awake and be sure to wash her face with a soft flannel dipped in tepid water once a day.

REFLEXES

Babies are born with dozens of reflex responses. One is the startle or Moro reflex, which means when she hears a loud noise or if her head isn't supported enough and tips backward, she'll throw her arms out and might even jerk a bit. Give her a soothing cuddle and all will be well again.

Two other reflexes are rooting for a nipple and sucking when the nipple is placed in his mouth. Another is a "walking" motion if you hold him upright. All these disappear in the first year as your baby gets control over his motions. At first, his movements will be jerky, but by the end of the first month, his body movements will smooth out and become more coordinated. That fist will make it into his mouth. She'll begin to stretch her arms and legs and arch her back.

THE FIVE SENSES

Babies this young don't focus well visually and their eyes are very sensitive to bright light. They can make eye contact only at close range—between 8–12 inches. His eyes may wander or cross. They prefer black-and-white patterns, as their color vision isn't fully mature yet. What they love to look at above all are human faces!

By the end of the first month, her hearing is fully developed. She will be able to recognize certain sounds and may turn toward your voice. And guess what? She can even remember some of what she hears.

You'll discover that she prefers sweet smells and can recognize the smell of your breast milk. She also likes soft sensations (like cuddly blankets) and gentle touch. Babies this young don't like rough handling. You want to hold her with a confident, firm hand without a lot of sudden motions!

SOCIAL/EMOTIONAL

Very young babies can get easily overstimulated. They literally don't know how to look away, for instance. If you find your baby getting cranky, it may very well be from too much stimulation. A quiet, dim room can do wonders for calming him down. You may find that he begins to comfort himself by mouthing and/or sucking his fist or fingers.

As the first month unfolds, you'll notice your baby becoming more alert and responsive. He'll listen when you talk, look at you when you're holding him, and might even move his body to get your attention or in response to something you do. You'll find his breathing may increase as you pick him up, particularly when it's feeding time. It's his way of saying *yes!*

Some time during the first thirty days or so, you'll get one of parents' greatest joys: your baby's first smile. It usually happens during sleep first. She may begin to gurgle too. You'll respond with a smile and a laugh of your own, and soon there will be a wonderful dance between you of sounds and smiles. Your responses to her tell your baby that you are with her, that how she feels matters, and are the very early basis for healthy self-esteem.

WHEN TO CALL THE DOCTOR

If by week three or so, you see any of the following:

- Feeds slowly and sucks poorly
- When a bright light is shined in face, doesn't blink
- No response to loud sounds
- Seems very stiff and unmoving or very floppy
- Constant lower jaw trembling even when not crying or excited

30–90 DAYS

You're going to see such development in this time! He's going to continue to gain 1½–2 pounds a month. His head will still grow more rapidly than the rest of his body. By the third month, the soft spot on his head will close. His bones grow quickly and he'll even develop muscles as he begins to move around more and the fat disappears.

Her neck will become stronger. When placed on her tummy, she'll begin to raise her head and chest to look around. She'll be able to flex and straighten her legs intentionally, and open and close her hands. He'll become much more active, spending lots of time watching his hands move. He may turn his head from side to side. Those fingers will start to come to her mouth and she'll be able to grasp things like your hair. (This one I know much about!)

Her visual range is expanding so that she can see your whole face, still her favorite toy. She'll learn how to track something moving in a half circle in front of her, and she'll be able to see at a distance, and in color. Eye-hand coordination begins to develop. She'll begin waving her arms up and down or around. She'll begin to make babbling sounds and respond to your voice. She'll start making facial expressions like frowning and lip pursing. Your baby is becoming social!

TEMPERAMENT

Yes, it's really true that babies come into the world with their own temperaments. Some are quiet, others active. Still others are cranky and easily startled. Some don't take change easily, others are more laid-back and roll with whatever's going on. Some sleep a lot, others not as much. That's one of the great things about being a parent—discovering just who this tiny being is who's been entrusted to your care. You don't get to order up the baby you want. Your job is to treasure the one you get. When you pay attention to the clues he drops in everything from eating to sleeping to crying, you'll begin to understand just who he is and how he bonds with you. I've had many a midwife be absolutely spot-on with intuitively knowing the temperament of a newborn. It's true you can just tell, yet it takes experience to know.

30–90 DAYS

As you spend time together, your baby's attachment to you increases immeasurably. As he gets to three months, he'll smile at the sound of your voice and when he sees your face. You may find he's more responsive to parents than any other adults,

WHEN TO CALL THE DOCTOR

If by three months, you are seeing the following:

- Doesn't grasp objects
- Doesn't smile
- Doesn't follow objects with eyes
- Eyes crossed most of the time or has trouble moving one or both eyes in all directions
- Doesn't babble
- Can't lift head while on tummy

but will likely become increasingly interested in other children and babies. You may find him mimicking other babies' facial expressions and sounds.

He recognizes your voice and is sensitive to your voice tone by now. Speak angrily around him and he'll probably cry. Talk sweetly and you'll get a smile. He's learning about your moods and personality at the same time you're learning about his. You may see him imitating your expressions and following your movement with his eyes. Your baby can sense so much from you.

Being able to smile as well as cry gives her another way to communicate with you, and you may find her smiling and babbling to get your attention. When you respond quickly and positively, you tell your baby that she's important to you, that she can express a need and get it satisfied, which helps in building self-trust now and self-esteem later on.

When you speak in response to a babble or a smile, he's beginning to learn that communication is a two-way process. Believe it or not, at this age he's beginning to learn many aspects of conversation, including voice tone, pace, and taking turns speaking.

His nervous system is developing and you'll find that he's better able to cope with frustrations than when first born. He may still have total meltdowns, but it's easier to soothe or distract him.

BABYPROOFING

When we think about making our homes safe, people usually think about electrical sockets, drowning, and falling. And of course we need to keep our babies safe from such hazards. But babyproofing encompasses so much more—it's really about creating a healthy environment so your baby can thrive.

In my experience, new parents tend to fall into one of two camps: the "nothing to worry about" crowd and "it's all so dangerous, it's a miracle any baby survives childhood" group. Both attitudes are problematic because they don't allow you to be realistic while doing as much as you can to prevent accidents. Life comes with hazards, especially for small babies, and it's important to prevent what we can. But we want to do it in such a way that doesn't breed hysteria or overwhelming fear in us or in our children.

By creating a safe environment but not being overly protective, we teach our children to take proper precautions as they grow and to know we can be counted on to keep them out of harm's way as much as possible. You're not looking to avoid every little bump, because that helps them learn dexterity and coordination, but to prevent serious emergencies. Better safe than sorry, right?

In Chapter 3, you've already learned about safe equipment and home furnishings to start with. As your baby goes through his first year, your safety concerns will change based on his growth and development. That's why I've included a special babyproofing section in each age period—to make sure you are paying attention to the crucial environmental and safety issues as your baby grows.

Each section builds upon the last. So for instance, when I suggest fire-retardant sleepwear or not leaving your baby alone with your pet in the first three months, it's meant to be a suggestion to carry through the whole year.

In babyproofing, I've written what I feel is the best for the *overall* safety of

INFANT FIRST AID

Because accidents happen despite our best intentions, I strongly urge you to take an infant first aid and CPR class immediately, if you haven't already. I've also included basic emergency first aid in Part 4. But this is not meant as a substitute for proper training.

children up to the age of one divided into age stages. To some of these you'll say, "That's not necessary for my child because they've already learned that." Or, "We don't actually need to have a lock there." Or, "We feel that this particular situation is fine. Our child is so petite she can't reach the stove." That makes sense. You will need to customize my recommendations to your living situation and your particular child. My suggestions are here to make you aware of what you need to consider and what you might need to do.

0–3 MONTHS

Remember what you learned about your baby's tiny lungs? They absorb twice as many airborne toxins as adults. So keeping her away from pollutants is key to keeping her breathing easy. That means keeping the air around her tobacco-free. Hopefully, you don't smoke. If you do, be sure to go outside. And enforce the outside rule for any visitors as well. Infants exposed to secondhand smoke have more colds, ear infections, are more likely to get asthma, pneumonia, bronchitis, and are at greater risk for sudden infant death syndrome (SIDS).

Keep floors and carpets clean—even at this young age, your baby will spend a lot of time on the floor on a blanket or bassinet. This is where heavier chemicals and small particles collect. Keep stairs and hallways free of objects that could trip you when you're carrying her.

BEDROOM

Make sure there is nothing above where your baby sleeps, like a shelf with knickknacks, which can fall down onto her. Don't leave her alone in your bed, and *never* put her on a water bed—it's too soft and can cause suffocation. Also, never cover her mattress with plastic. That is also a smothering hazard.

Never put necklaces, cords attached to pacifiers, or any kind of cord around his neck. If you use an electrical space heater or night-light, make sure it's not near bedding or drapes, to prevent a fire. Be sure to put your baby in fire-retardant sleepwear at bedtime. By law, all pajamas are.

Never leave her unattended on the changing table. You never know when she'll learn to roll over. Things happen suddenly. One minute she can't do something and the next minute, boom!

BATHROOM

Never leave a baby alone in the tub, even for a second, even if he's in a bathtub seat. The suction cups can come loose and he can fall facedown. Turn the hot water heater setting down to the lowest setting and always test the water with your elbow before putting him in to avoid burns. Why the elbow, you may ask? Because our hands are used to being in a lot warmer temperatures and so are less sensitive. There are also bath thermometers you can buy. Store all electrical appliances such as hair dryers, curling irons, electric toothbrushes, etc. away from tub or sink to prevent electrocution.

KITCHEN

Don't hold your baby while cooking or drinking hot liquids. She can get burned. Place her in the bassinet a few feet away from you. Or place her in her little bouncy seat or the baby gym, so she's having fun stretching out, grabbing the mirror and the little dangly features above her while you're having coffee. I remember many coffee mornings, when a group of moms and nannies got their babies together. The babies were in the middle of the room playing and the moms and nannies were around the edges drinking their coffee.

If you're heating bottles, it's recommended that you put the bottle in a pan of water on the stove rather than use the microwave because microwaves heat unevenly and you can end up scalding him. However, I believe in being realistic and some people will use the microwave because it's very, very quick. Thirty seconds and you've got a warm bottle. Shake it well after heating to avoid hot spots and test on the back of your wrist. Then leave it for a bit before you feed your baby. It's proper common sense.

Keep a list of emergency numbers in the room you're mostly going to be in like the kitchen or the family room so it's at your fingertips—911, the pediatrician, poison control. You can post them on a big corkboard, along with other useful info.

CAR

You already know that your baby must be in a rear-facing car seat every time you drive. But also think about what you put next to him in the car. Keep grocery bags and other heavy items in the trunk so that if you come to a quick stop or are hit, he won't be injured by flying objects. If you must have them in the car, put them on the floor of the front seat.

Tragic news has been reported of parents who have forgotten their infant in the backseat of the car on a hot day, which is very dangerous and can lead to death. One way to remember is to put a sticky note on your dash every time you take her with you. Or put a stuffed animal in the front seat when she's in the back.

To keep the car cool and to protect your baby from the sun while driving, you can get those suction window shades. In a pinch, I've rolled down the window a bit, put a towel up and then rolled up the window. Putting towels on the seats keeps them cooler as well. Park in a shady spot even if it means walking farther.

QUICK SUN PROTECTION

Sun is not only dangerous to baby's skin, but also their eyes. Whenever I'm outside with a newborn, I always put a cloth diaper over the seat or stroller for instant sun protection. It's cotton so it can breathe and allows air but not sun to penetrate. I find it easier than fussing with carriage shades or umbrellas if I'm getting in and out of cars.

Protect your baby from the sun totally at this stage because you shouldn't use sunscreen until he's six months old. Use carriage shades, umbrellas, and a hat with a wide brim and tail that will shade his face and the back of his neck. I call them the Foreign Legion caps. Avoid being outside during the hours of 11:00 AM–3:00 PM if at all possible, and if you live somewhere extremely hot, daylight hours altogether. Damp baby down continuously with a wet cloth.

PETS

Never leave your baby alone in a room with a pet. Pets can get very jealous and do unpredictable things, even the most gentle ones. When your baby is very young, avoid having the pet go near your baby at all. Distance is best for the first year. To your pet, this tiny creature is a stranger—one that makes a lot of noise and smells funny. As your baby gets older, he may unintentionally provoke the pet by pulling the tail or grabbing fur. Be aware also that pets can cause allergies. I know this firsthand! And separation helps prevent pets from giving ticks, ringworm, and other unpleasantries to your baby. Especially if your baby has asthma or was born with eczema.

If you are thinking of getting a pet, wait until your child is older. If you already have one, and if you think it will be a burden to manage the animal as well as your newborn, consider boarding it for the first week or two or having a friend take it. If you don't think it's going to be a burden that's because I'm assuming that you and your partner have sat down to work out who's going to take care of the animal, and together you're going to be responsible for not leaving your baby in a room where the animal is. Consider a baby gate to keep them separated. And never tie a dog's leash to the stroller while walking—the dog can tip it over!

SHAKEN BABY SYNDROME

No matter how frustrated, annoyed, impatient or angry you get, never shake your baby. It can permanently damage his brain and spinal cord, causing blindness, paralysis, and death. As I expressed before, if he won't stop crying and it's getting on your last nerve, put him down in his basket and take a breather in another room. Call a friend or relative for help, or a parent help hotline. (See resources in Part 4.)

I've put this warning in a couple places because parents feel the need to have to control their baby's crying. And the feeling of helplessness that arises when you can't leads to frustration that can then lead to anger. It's important to understand this, because the more you understand that you can't control your baby's crying and that what you need at certain times is patience, the less frustrated you'll feel.

SETTING FIRM GROUND

Setting firm ground is about creating healthy routines of waking, sleeping, and stimulating play, as well as dealing effectively with crying. I can't emphasise enough the importance of routines. The more you can create routines early on, the easier your life will be—not just this first year, but throughout your baby's childhood. Routine creates security and stability for your baby and for you. You both feel less overwhelmed, and routines utilize time well so you can do other things too.

This is not to say that you must rigidly make your baby follow a schedule. But I strongly believe that being a good parent is about being able both to create routines and stay flexible. It's the middle ground—not too rigid and not too loose. That takes practice.

For instance, say your baby is now three months old and usually has a nap in his crib at 1:00. You're out having lunch with a friend. Do you have to rush home to keep to the schedule if he's drifting off in his stroller? That's too rigid. I'm not a stickler for "must sleep at the same time in the same place every day." But it is about making sure to create and follow a consistent pattern of sleeping and feeding. After all, if he's asleep in a stroller, he's on schedule, just in a different place.

Routines

In the beginning, your baby sleeps so much and feeds so often that, especially if you have other children, it is easier to maintain your previous routine and fit the new baby into that. After a while, however, as he is more alert, things are going to have to fit around the baby. Your number-one priority this year is making sure that your baby's needs for sleep, food, and stimulation are met, because he's totally dependent on you. That takes good time management, particularly if you've got more than one child.

I'm a big fan of keeping a baby log for the first eight weeks. That's why I've provided space in the back of this book. It's a way of tracking when he's sleeping and when awake, so that you can begin to see patterns and create routines that will work for you when he's a bit older.

Sleeping

One of the main developmental tasks of the first year is to sleep. That's because the proper amount of sleep is critical to healthy physical and mental development. The National Sleep Foundation recommends 10.5–18 hours of sleep per day for infants up to three months, and I agree. So you should be doing all you can to make that easy and safe.

Rule number one: Always put her to sleep on her back on firm bedding to reduce the possibility of sudden infant death syndrome (SIDS). Babies who sleep on their tummies have a twenty-one times higher risk of SIDS. And make sure she's not overbundled at night. That's also been associated with SIDS. See the diagram for two safe sleeping positions—flat on back or one shoulder elevated, which works for a very refluxy baby.

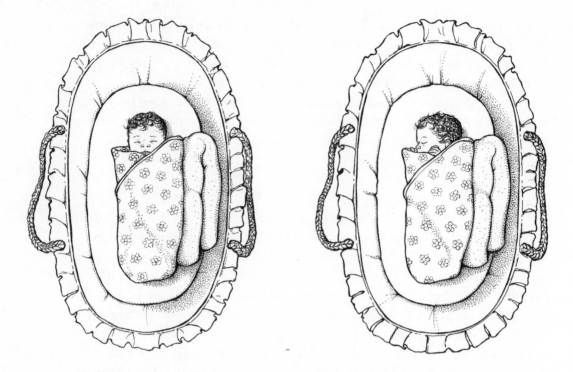

During the first three months, it's really not necessary to have your baby sleeping in a bedroom when they take those naps, although it's good practice for you. If she falls asleep in her bouncing seat, fair enough. It's important for your baby to fall asleep listening to house noises around her to get used to a certain amount of noise while sleeping. Now, I'm not suggesting that as soon as your baby falls off to sleep you put the vacuum cleaner on, but that you don't have to have complete silence. You want a resilient, adaptable baby who doesn't have to have a blackout-blinds room to fall asleep. That tends to create a baby who may have trouble going to sleep in other places and settings.

If you are using a crib right away, make sure that the bottom half of the crib is made up with the blankets that are placed just up to your baby's tummy and no higher. If you put her at the top, she can wriggle down and suffocate. At the bottom, she's got nowhere to go. Also, never use quilts in the bassinet or crib. Babies can get caught underneath them, which could be fatal.

BEDDING TRICK

To save on changing bedding all the time, put on a fitted sheet, take a cloth diaper and put it over the head part of the bassinet or crib. Then wrap it and tuck it tightly in so when you put her down on her back with her head to the side after she feeds, she'll dribble on the diaper, not the bottom sheet, and you'll only have to change that.

Medical experts don't recommend sleeping with infants, as you can accidentally roll over in your sleep and suffocate them. Also, your body heat can cause them to get overheated. (Of course, you can have them sleep in your arms after feeding, which is a wonderful aspect of bonding.) I also discourage infants regularly sleeping in your bed because you're creating a habit that will cause you no end of grief later on. As a nanny, I've had to troubleshoot many toddlers who are so used to sleeping in their parents' bed that they know no different. Getting them off to sleep in their own bed has become a real problem. I want you to create good sleeping habits from the beginning. That's why this section is called Setting Firm Ground.

Whether he sleeps in your room in his bassinet or his own, don't expect your baby to sleep through the night until he's on solid foods. His tummy just gets empty too fast. As your infant reaches the three-month mark, he may take a late feed at midnight and sleep right through to the morning. Hallelujah! That means you get a good night's sleep too! But that will not likely consistently be true until solids are introduced.

That's why this is not yet the time to create a firm bedtime policy, because your baby will likely be crying for lack of food. No matter how many times she cries during this period, you need to offer food and check the diaper. It's only four months or so to get through.

Swaddling

When your baby is newborn, because he's been so tightly compacted into the womb, swaddling him to go to sleep will help him feel secure. But when a baby

is awake, it's important for him to have space and to be able to kick his feet around and see where his toes and hands are. So I don't recommend keeping your newborn tightly wrapped when awake, unless he's very irritable without it. And if you find your baby doesn't like to be swaddled to sleep, don't do it. You can experiment by trying it each way for a few days and see which works best.

To swaddle, fold up a blanket into a triangle shape with the longer length at the top, reaching your baby's shoulders and then very neatly placing one angle or point right across in an angular way across your baby's body. Tuck that underneath by his legs and then put the bottom tip up toward his tummy, then cross over with the other angle and underneath the legs. (See diagram.)

Some babies like to have their arms out, and others like to have them tucked in. Try it both ways and you'll see which your baby prefers.

As your baby gets older you may want to move away from the swaddling and use a baby's sleep bag. I love them. You can get ones for the summer that are lightweight and quilted ones for the winter.

Remember, however, to be careful not to overheat your baby. Make sure the room is not overheated, as well. You want to be able to take the chill off the room without drying it out too much. If the room is very dry and stuffy from central heating, place some water bowls on top of the radiators to moisten the air or get a humidifier.

Getting Baby Off to Sleep

Many babies fall asleep to a musical mobile hanging over the bassinet or crib. And that's fine. I've found, however, in the beginning that nothing beats rocking, babe in arms. You'll find you'll make your own tune and move accordingly to that. It's the repetition that works, but make sure you're not making your baby or yourself dizzy by swinging around like the teacups at Disneyland. Gentle! And soft singing. This is about going to sleep, not revving up.

Sleep Patterns

Every baby is different. Below I show you one baby's sleeping pattern from newborn to four weeks and from 4–6 weeks, to give you a rough idea of what you might expect. But remember, no two babies are alike.

SETTING DOWN A SLEEPING BABY

When he falls asleep in your arms and you want to set him down without waking him up, move slowly. Gently lay his head down first, then put the rest of his body down so he's on his back with your hands still under him. Gradually take away one hand, then the other, pausing after each to give him a chance to settle. Then stand next to him for a minute or two so that you can pat him or make soothing noises in case he stirs.

NEWBORN–4 WEEKS		4–6 WEEKS	
Time	Activity	Time	Activity
7:00 AM	awake	6:00 AM	awake
	daytime sleep		daytime sleep
9:00 PM–2:00 AM	awake	6:30 PM	asleep
3:00 AM–7:00 AM	asleep	10:00 PM–1:00 AM	awake
		1:00 AM–6:00 AM	asleep

My Pacifier Philosophy

I like to give a newborn a pacifier when she goes to sleep. Here's why: babies' instinct is to suck and then fall asleep. If you give her something to suck on, she'll fall asleep more easily because the association is there. So a pacifier is a sleep aid. However, not every baby likes a pacifier so check it out.

As babies become older, that pacifier becomes something that they literally take into their own hands to soothe themselves. So it has a use as a sleep aid and for self soothing.

However, pacifiers are being misused. They're used by parents when their baby is awake to stop her from making noise rather than thinking about what she might need for stimulation or comfort. They are also used for too long. No baby should go past a year with a pacifier and the sooner she can sleep without one, the better. Overuse of pacifiers can cause a child not to learn other ways to comfort herself. It also arches the mouth and can cause mouth sores and buck teeth, and delay speech. So wean it away at no later than twelve months during the day and eighteen months at night.

If you use a pacifier, make sure it's kept clean because it can obviously collect a lot of germs. Wash it out by hand with lukewarm water and very mild soap, and rinse thoroughly. If you put it in the dishwasher or the sterilizer, the rubber becomes scalded.

Learning Your Baby's Cries

Crying is how babies communicate when they're hungry, tired, afraid, bored, frustrated, overwhelmed, wet, cold, hot, in pain . . . Life outside the womb is stressful, and it takes a while to adjust to it. Soon he'll get used to life in the big, exciting world and be less stressed, and you'll get better at understanding and meeting his needs.

Work out why your baby's crying. What does that cry mean? And that tone within that cry? Is it sporadic? What's the pitch? Pay attention and you'll start getting an intuitive knowingness: "Oh, that's because she's hungry. The last time she fed was two hours ago, and I've just changed the diaper . . ." This is what I call the elimination period where you go through all the things it can't be. The more you do it, the quicker your brain becomes at checking things off.

When babies are young, they are not crying to manipulate, irritate, or annoy you. In toddlerhood, which is when I suggest active ignoring in certain circumstances, is when you see 3–4-year-olds trying to get their own way. With babies, they are trying to express some real need and so you should try, as much as possible, to figure out and respond to that need, understanding that some babies have very sensitive nervous systems. They may be communicating *ouch!* and there may not be much you can do. The more you pay attention, the more you'll learn what your baby's cries mean.

Some babies cry until they gag. They might be having a temper tantrum, which escalates to a point that the baby doesn't even know why she's crying. And that may cause a spasm when they gag. Just clean up the mess and try to calm her down as best as possible.

FEEDING

Your Baby's Food Needs

Whether you breast-feed or not, breast milk or formula is all your baby needs for the first three months. Giving a baby solid foods before four months or so, when his digestive tract

DEALING WITH CRYING NEWBORNS

It will be one of these, unless she's sickly:

- Check the diaper first and then offer food.
- If he's dry and full, try movement: walking, rocking, jiggling, swaying, patting.
- Put her close to your heart. She's used to hearing that in the womb.
- Sing or hum softly or turn on soothing music. Experiment to see which works best. Your voice, because he's heard it in the womb, is often best, especially with lots of tiny kisses.
- Try white noise—a clothes dryer, vacuum, or one of those fancy machines.
- See if swaddling helps.
- Put her in her seat or gym; maybe she's bored.
- Have your partner try.

is not properly developed, can result in allergies and digestive problems. If he's hungry, give more breast milk or formula. Never, never give cow's milk, even if you dilute it with water. It has far too much protein for infants to absorb.

I'm in favor of demand feeding for the first few weeks—letting your baby feed whenever she wants to. If he doesn't cry, that doesn't mean he's not hungry. In general, newborns feed as much as every two hours, or 8–10 times a day in the beginning. If you're bottle feeding, that's 8–10 bottles of 2–4 ounces each. Don't worry—his tummy will grow and he'll need to feed less often!

When you are at about week four, see my suggestions for beginning to establish a feeding routine on page 95. For right now, just as you did for sleeping, I want you to record in the baby log at the back of the book the times he feeds, as

FEEDING TROUBLESHOOTING

- Babies hiccup, even in the womb. If he's really hungry or upset when being fed, he tends to hiccup more. If he hiccups while being fed, just take out the nipple, burp him, and wait for the hiccups to pass.
- If she falls asleep while feeding, blow gently on her face to wake her, especially if she's a preemie or underfeeding and you want to get some nourishment into her. Or put a little damp cloth over her if it's hot.
- Babies have a tendency to spit up after feeding (reflux), which can freak you out if it's a lot the first time. It's normal, because their esophagus muscle is not yet fully developed. They usually do it because they've either had too much to eat or swallowed too much air.
- If she spits up a lot: feed your baby before she's starving; burp her more often; feed in a quiet, calm place; keep a clean cotton diaper on your shoulder to wipe up and wear clothes you don't care about getting messy. Keep her upright right after feeding. Put her in an infant seat to sleep. If you're bottle feeding, make sure the hole is neither too little (too much air) or too big (too much formula). You want a one-hole slow nipple, so they get small amounts often. Ditto with preemies.
- Don't worry too much about spitting up unless your baby is listless, has trouble breathing, has projectile vomit, or if the spit-up is green (bile) or has blood in it. If any of these symptoms are present, see a doctor immediately.
- If you're bottle-feeding, every baby likes the bottle at different temperatures so experiment to find out what yours likes.

this will help you form a routine when it's time. Keeping a baby log is also a way to figure out if what you're eating may be causing gas—"Oh, I had Thai last night, and he's had a horrible day."

Babies grow in spurts throughout the whole of the first year, typically at three weeks, 6–8 weeks, three months, and six months. You'll know yours is having a growth spurt because he'll suddenly be much hungrier and will feed more.

Breast-feeding

Guess what? Breast-feeding doesn't come naturally—at least to many moms. Don't worry too much if it takes you a while to get the hang of it or if you're going along just fine and then run into trouble. The more you stress, the less it's likely to work right. Your community midwife is available to help night or day. Common problems include the baby not latching on properly (more on that later), and a milk supply out of sync with the baby's needs. It can take up to a month to establish a good routine. And if you find it too emotionally or physically exhausting, remember bottle-feeding isn't the end of the world. But I wouldn't give up breast-feeding straightaway. A baby can take both.

And guess what? Nature has designed it that your breasts will produce more milk in response to your baby sucking. So the supply should, in general, meet demand if you let your baby feed whenever he wants. Unless told by your doctor or home visitor, don't supplement with formula for at least six weeks to take advantage of this supply-and-demand effect. You most likely will produce enough, if—and it's a big *if*—you take good care of yourself. You can only make enough milk if you eat properly, drink plenty of water and other fluids, and get enough sleep. You'll be surprised how intense your hunger and thirst will be! Breast-feeding is calorie burning so you need to refuel.

Stress also can reduce your milk supply, so you want to create as peaceful an environment as possible. That's why I recommend having lots of help and not striving for domestic perfection. You need to take care of yourself so you can feed your baby. Do what you know chills you out so that you can get enough rest. One disguised blessing of a C-section is that it forces you to sleep, or at least rest!

Eating for Two

What you eat will get into your baby's body through your milk. That's why it's recommended that you avoid caffeine and alcohol, as well as prescription or over-the-counter medicines unless prescribed by your doctor. Strong or acidic foods can make your milk smell funny and cause your infant indigestion or refusal to nurse. Gassy foods, like broccoli, beans, cabbage, etc. can produce gas in your baby too. So can dairy products. These are generalizations; every baby is different. You'll find out yourself soon enough when she reacts.

I don't believe you have to eat really bland stuff just because you're breast-feeding. Here's my suggestion: Eat whatever you want and if there's a reaction in your baby, cut that food out. Or live with the consequences and know your baby's living with them too. One exception—do keep alcohol and caffeine intake low, as in none. I'm not saying one-half glass of champagne to celebrate your baby's birth is a no-no. But in general, steer clear. Your baby's brain doesn't need it!

It takes about 4–6 hours for something you ate to make its way to your milk so take that into account when you're trying to figure out a food culprit. And don't eliminate everything at once or you won't be able to tell which food is causing the trouble.

Make sure you're getting enough calcium, iron, vitamin D, folic acid, and other nutrients through healthy food choices. Go for healthy meals and snacks as much as possible. That means lots of fruits and veggies a day. You need an extra 550 calories to produce enough milk for one baby. Stay away from shark, tuna, mackerel, tilefish, and swordfish as studies show they are high in mercury and other pollutants that can find their way to your baby's brain.

Breast Milk

At first, your breasts produce something called *colostrum*, which is a watery fluid that is sometimes yellow and contains important antibodies. It serves as a laxative to eliminate the black tarry waste in your baby's bowels called *meconium* that he produced before birth. At about day three, you begin to make "transitional milk," which is the shift from colostrum to milk, which has less protein and antibodies than colostrum, and more fat, calories, and lactose (a form of sugar). In a few days more, you'll be producing mature milk, high in lactose and low in protein, which is what your baby needs to help her immature digestive system maximize calcium intake and other nutrients.

As your milk comes in, you may experience a tremendous amount of teariness, which is a result of hormone shifts. It's so common it has a name—"three day" or "baby" blues. It may also be painful—something like the feeling of heavy, achy hotness in your breasts. Now your milk will appear thin and bluish white, particularly at the beginning of each feed. As your baby feeds, the flow will slow as the amount of fat increases. Nature designed it this way to quench a baby's thirst first and then provide more fat so she gets food and drink at each meal.

Step-by-Step Breast-feeding

GETTING IN POSITION

First, make yourself comfortable sitting in bed or a chair. Support your back and put the *V* pillow around your lap and on to the bottom of your belly. If you have large breasts, take a rolled-up flannel and tuck it under the breast you'll nurse first with. Then pick up the baby and turn her head toward your tummy, with her bottom toward your other elbow and your arm cradling her body and resting against the pillow to help you bear her weight. Bring her up to your breast rather than you leaning down so you don't strain your back or put pressure on your incision. You can also use the lying-down position shown below.

LATCHING ON

Place her nose opposite your nipple for accurate positioning. Allow her head to naturally tilt back as she begins to open her mouth wide with you still holding her neck for support. Squeeze a drop of colostrum or milk out of the nipple and brush her lips with the nipple and quickly bring her to your breast. Her bottom lip and chin should touch your breast first thing. As she latches on, you should feel the letdown, a sensation like a blood pressure cuff around your breast. It should go away within thirty seconds or so. And even if you're doing it right, until your nipples get used to it, they may feel a bit sore.

When she's latched on properly, her lips form a seal and at least one-third of the dark area around the nipple (the aureola) will be in her mouth. She needs to suck here in order to receive milk. If she only sucks the nipple itself, she will not drain the breast well and you may end up with painful cracked nipples and a buildup of milk in the ducts, which can lead to mastitis, a painful infection. If she only has your nipple, break the suction with your finger and try again. Never try to pull her off—that will hurt. Always break the seal with your finger.

Once she's latched on, listen to hear sucking and swallowing noises. You've done it! This position allows your baby to breathe and feed while you support her and yourself comfortably.

Switch to the other breast when it seems like the first is drained. You can tell by not seeing sucking or hearing swallowing. You can't judge by time exactly because it varies widely from baby to baby—as little as ten minutes or up to forty, depending if she's a slow or fast feeder. Before you switch, be sure to burp her. (See description on pages 92–93.) It's okay if she only feeds on one breast. Next time, offer the other first.

NURSING NEED-TO-KNOWS

You'll find your baby will have his own nursing style. Some are gobblers, others are dawdlers. Some pause to sleep, then feed again. Some get frantic at the smell of the breast and have a hard time latching on. Others knead and tug at you while nursing. Then there are those who feed, throw up half of it on to you, and then need to feed immediately again. Is this sounding familiar? Remember—your baby is unique. Discovering and treasuring that uniqueness is one of the joys of parenting. Yes, even having to change him several times a day as if doing a fashion show due to reflux!

You might discover that your baby takes to one breast over the other. If so, start him on the unfavored breast when he's the most hungry. That way your milk won't dry up there and you won't end up feeling lopsided!

If your baby latches on fine and then pulls off crying after a couple of minutes, it may be that the milk is coming too fast for him to swallow. It sounds like when fluid goes down the wrong pipe in adults. Try expressing some or pumping before he feeds. If that doesn't solve the problem, it could be something you ate or he's got a cold and can't breathe out of his nose, or he has an earache. If you've checked out those possibilities, it could be a passing mood. Eventually he'll get hungry enough to eat. And get support if you have questions or concerns. Direct help lines to immediate help are preferable. Don't suffer in silence! Sometimes babies can just get a bit fussy until feeding is in full flow.

There's controversy over whether women should be breast-feeding in public. I think that's neither here nor there. What's important is making sure that you're in a place where you feel relaxed so you can just glow with your milk supply and are able to breast-feed your baby. If you want to be alone, fine. Do what's comfortable to you!

If you are breast-feeding out and about, slings are great. All you have to do is adjust it so your baby's head is at your breast, latch him on and hold him with the opposite arm. You can even adjust the fabric so no one can see.

One thing that makes mothers anxious when breast-feeding is that you can't see how much milk your baby is getting. Here's how to tell all is well. After the first week, she should:

- have 6–8 wet diapers a day (pour 2 ounces of water into a diaper to get an idea).
- gain weight. (Remember, babies lose weight the first week.)
- have poop that looks like cottage cheese mixed with dark mustard.
- be alert and responsive when awake and sleep contentedly.
- not be throwing up too much.
- stay on the breast, breathing and sucking hard for thirty minutes.

PUMPING MILK

As I said earlier, I'm not opposed to pumping breast milk because it gives moms relief and rest, particularly in the late evening and early morning feeds, and gives dads the chance to bond with their babies during feeding. It will also give moms the opportunity to go out once in a while on her own.

I suggest beginning at around 4–6 weeks. Before then, unless you pump regularly, it may affect the quantity of your milk supply. After that, you may encounter resistance to an artificial nipple from your baby or he may refuse the breast. To make it easier, pump on one side while the baby is feeding on the other if you can.

Have someone other than Mom bottle-feed. What's confusing to an infant is to have a bottle put in his mouth when he can smell the real deal right there. Try it for the first time when he's really hungry. Squeeze out a couple drops and rub on his lips, then place the nipple slowly into his mouth. If you're having trouble with him accepting it, try holding him in a different position than the one he's used to with breast-feeding. I doubt he will refuse as young as he is, because of the survival instinct, but for older babies, weaning to a bottle takes persistence.

If you can't pump while feeding, pump at the same time each day, at least one

BREAST CARE

- Make sure your hands are clean before nursing.
- Use an ice pack on your nipples before nursing. This will not only reduce pain but will help them stand up, which aids in latching on.
- Avoid soap on the nipples. After nursing, wash them in a teaspoon of vinegar diluted with a cup of water to sterilize and then air-dry to prevent cracking.
- Sore nipples? Place cool used tea bags on each for a couple minutes. You can also dab with a bit of breast milk.
- Leaks happen—usually in the first weeks. It can occur when you hear a baby cry, have sex, are about to feed your baby. . . . If it's bothersome, wear breast pads or a thick cotton bra.
- When you feel the tingle that means your milk is about to let down and it's an inappropriate time, press your breasts tightly with your arm and you may be able to avoid a leak.
- If your nipples are painful, pump milk for a day and give them a rest.
- Use a front latching nursing bra so it's easy to get free and feed and never wear one with an underwire—studies have shown they contribute to plugged milk ducts.

hour after she's fed and one hour before she's likely to again, and whenever your baby doesn't drain both breasts. In the beginning, you may find the quantity is low, until your breasts start producing more to meet the increased demand. Remember this quote: "More rest is best, for you will have more milk to ingest."

CARE AND HANDLING OF PUMPED MILK

Breast milk will last at room temp for six hours, in the fridge for eight days, the freezer for two weeks, and the deep freeze for up to three months. Once you thaw it, it should be consumed within twenty-four hours if stored in the fridge. Do not refreeze. Store it in 2–4-ounce portions in small zipper plastic bags that you record the date and amount on. To defrost, use warm, not hot, running water or you will kill the antibodies in the milk. Shake well after you put it in a bottle as the fat will have risen to the top.

BOTTLE-FEEDING

Bottle-feeding makes it easy for Dad and others to help out round-the-clock. There are so many bottle types out there now! You have the choice of glass, plastic, or plastic bottles with throwaway inserts. I prefer the plastic ones because they tend to produce fewer air bubbles and are easier to clean. The inserts also prevent air bubbles but they must have the air squeezed out of them when filling.

Eliminating air bubbles is important because the trick to bottle-feeding is to make sure that your baby gets enough milk without getting too much air. Otherwise she'll be gassy and uncomfortable. If you find gas a real problem, consider a bottle with a slow flow tube.

What's also really important is having the right kind of nipples, as I suggested in Chapter 3. The hole should be big enough to allow a few drops per second and the nipple should mimic a natural one—wide and big enough so your infant can latch on properly. Some nipples come with more than one hole for small, medium, and fast

WHEN TO CALL THE DOCTOR

Breast infections can happen and are serious. Be sure to get medical care immediately if:

- You have a fever or feel like you have the flu.
- Your breasts are hot and painfully hard (as opposed to full).
- You feel a hard lump or pain in the breast (it may only be a clogged milk duct that can be treated with heat and massage, but it's best to get it checked out).
- Red patches or streaks appear on your breast.
- Your nipples are cracked and burn whenever your baby nurses (you could have thrush).

Keep nursing until you are seen. Stopping will actually make the infection worse. One common infection is mastitis. It can be treated with antibiotics and breast-feeding to clear the ducts, but will leave you in tears and your baby may get an upset tummy from the medication.

flow. If your baby is getting a lot of air, lower the nipple size or have stops in between if he gets frustrated if it's not coming fast enough. The brown latex teats are the nearest you'll get to a nipple, but I prefer the clear ones as they are slightly firmer. It's easier to see if they're clean because they're see-through, and there is more durability with them.

FORMULA TIPS

- Formulas are either milk- or soy-based. Research has shown that soy doesn't reduce risk of allergies (in fact, many babies are allergic to soy) or colic. So choose one and if your baby has troubles—vomits a lot, has lots of diarrhea, and/or develops a red rash on her bottom or face—switch. Make sure whatever you use is iron fortified.

- Formulas come in powders, liquid concentrates, and ready to serve. Open powders stay fresh for a month if covered and stored in a cool, dry place. Store open cans or cartons of liquids in the coldest part of the fridge and do not keep for more than twenty-four hours.

- Make sure you wash your hands, the counter, and the top of the can before opening.

- If you're using powder or liquid concentrate, make sure to follow directions exactly. With powder, use the scoop and level it with a knife. Use a liquid measuring cup for the water to make sure the water level is correct. The right percentage is crucial. Too much formula will create constipation and pain. Too much water, your baby is not getting enough nutrients.

- When filling bottles, keep the nipple and cap in the sterilizer until ready to put on. Shake well to avoid lumps.

- There's no need to heat formula—room temperature is fine. If your baby prefers it warm, heat bottle in saucepan of water on the stove. Don't microwave, which can cause uneven heating and might burn her. It also continues to heat after it's been taken out. If you must microwave, do it when she's at least six months old, shake well, and test a few drops on your wrist to make sure it's not too hot.

- After a few days when you figure out how many bottles he uses, make them up all at once rather than having to do it when he's crying. It saves time and is good preparation.

- If she doesn't finish a bottle, throw the rest away. Formula quickly breeds bacteria.

STERILIZING SHOULDS

Although it is said that it's okay to use a dishwasher for bottles from birth, I like to use a sterilizer for at least six months as it keeps them hygienically clean. Sterilizers properly used reduce the chances of sickness and diarrhea.

■ Clean with hot water and soap, and rinse with hot water before sterilizing.

■ If you use a cold water sterilizer, every twenty-four hours leave equipment in sterilizing solution for at least thirty minutes. Beware that some cold water sterilizers can cause thrush in baby's mouth if not rinsed properly before use. So always rinse bottle after sterilizing in cool boiled water before using.

■ If using a steam sterilizer, make sure bottles and nipples are facing down in the sterilizer. Any bottles not being used and left standing should be sterilized again. Be sure to rinse bottles after sterilizing in cool boiled water before using.

BOTTLE-FEEDING POSITION

Sit down and cradle him in one arm. (See diagram.) Put a *V* pillow under that arm and around your body for support. Hold him at a 45–degree angle so his ears are higher than his mouth and chin is out a bit. Never hold him completely flat while feeding or you can cause formula to get into his eustacian tubes and develop into an ear infection. Hold the bottle firmly with your free hand, squeeze out a couple drops of formula, and touch your baby's cheek that's closest to your body. When he turns toward you, touch his lips with the nipple and slowly put it into his mouth. Make sure the tip is all the way back and up on the palate.

To minimize burping, keep adjusting the angle of the bottle as he feeds to keep the nipple full of formula. However, don't tip the bottle up more than necessary because that will cause the formula to come out too fast and cause the baby to gulp in more air and milk. If he takes in too much air, he might end up making choking noises and burping up the whole bottle. If he slows down, burp him and try again, but don't force it. Hold the bottle, but allow room to move the hand holding it. Babies will get into a

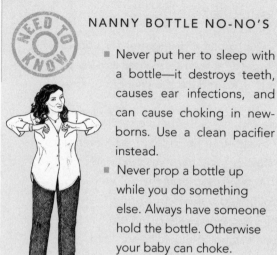

NANNY BOTTLE NO-NO'S

- Never put her to sleep with a bottle—it destroys teeth, causes ear infections, and can cause choking in newborns. Use a clean pacifier instead.
- Never prop a bottle up while you do something else. Always have someone hold the bottle. Otherwise your baby can choke.

rhythm when feeding to allow maximum flow and breathing without stopping.

DIAPER CHECK

Bottle-fed babies move their bowels much less frequently than breast-fed babies (it can be as little as once every two or three days, although I've never been that lucky) and their stools are usually more tan and solid. They're not constipated unless their stools are hard. Breast-fed babies may go as often as they eat and have runny, grainy, mustardy-looking poo. Green stools are also common. You may hear explosive sounds. Those are normal, and certainly break the silence in a crowd! Just keep plenty of diapers and clean clothes around. When babies begin on solid foods, their stools firm up and, with breast-fed babies, become less frequent. If you see black, white, or red stools, or if they are very watery or pale, consult your doctor or health visitor.

If your baby is constipated a lot or has excess diarrhea, assess how long it's been going on. Is it related to diet? Some parents don't follow the formula instructions properly and make too strong a bottle—too much powder. That can cause constipation. Or perhaps it's the kind of formula you're using. Your baby could be allergic, which causes diarrhea. Switch to a different one.

In the case of constipation, for immediate relief try a warm bath. If the problem persists, talk to the doctor.

BURPING

When babies feed, they take in air as well as milk or formula. That's why they have to be burped—to get rid of air bubbles that can cause gas. Gas can also be caused in breast-feeding babies by Mom's diet. Gas is an issue because it causes pain, which can result in a howling baby.

To minimize gas pains, burp your baby in the middle of his feeding (or more of-

ten if he's particularly gassy), as well as after. I've found three methods to be particularly successful. The first is over the shoulder. (See figure at right.) Your baby is close to upright and you gently pat his upper back.

The second is to sit him on your lap facing you and just give the tiniest turn one way and then the other to release the air pockets. (See next three figures.)

The third is on his side with one hand under him. He's slightly leaning over and you rock him. (See figure on following page.) This one is particularly good if he is colicky because the pressure on his tummy is very soothing.

Water just slightly warmer than tepid is also very good for getting rid of burping. Just put it in a bottle. It helps the air bubbles to burst. Make sure you give only 1–3 ounces and not before he's three months. Water intoxication is real and can be deadly.

There's nothing worse than a baby howling in pain from gas. In addition to burping position number 3, try massaging her tummy, giving warm baths, and, as much as you can, distract her with some kind of calm stimulation. See my suggestions for colicky babies below. Some babies have favorite songs that do the trick to distract. Singing and rocking can help. Sometimes, when a baby's in pain, it's awful, because they're so helpless and you're so helpless. Ride with it, knowing it will end, like teething.

COLIC

Colic is crying that lasts for at least two hours at certain times of the day (usually late evenings) and happens at least three times a week. It begins in the first month. It was thought to be caused by gas, but some medical experts now think it's the result of an immature nervous system that is easily irritated. Try the burping remedies I suggested. If that doesn't work, try:

- putting him next to a white noise machine or vibrating noises like clothes dryers, or take him for a ride in the car
- repetitive rocking movements
- carrying him tight across your body
- giving a pacifier to suck
- rocking or dancing with him

- various music to find a song that works
- taking turns with your partner

I promise you he'll grow out of it, usually around the fourth month, which is hard to remember when he's wailing for the fourth hour today. Whatever you do, remember, don't shake him in frustration. That can cause brain damage or death. If you're losing control or patience, take a break. If no one is there, put him down in his bassinet and go into another room. Call a friend or a hotline and talk about how you're feeling until you're calm again.

If you have a colicky baby, be sure to line up lots of help: spouse, friends, relatives. There are also help lines listed in the resource guide. Constant crying is not something one person should endure by herself! It can bring you and your partner to desperation. But know you can only do what you can and as long as he has you to hold him, he has his parents' love while this is happening, which is a very good thing.

ESTABLISHING A FEEDING ROUTINE

At about week 4, you can begin to establish a feeding routine. This is important because otherwise, your baby can overfeed, whether being breast- or bottle-fed. Babies also suck for comfort as well as hunger and if you offer food every time they cry, they can end up eating too much and become more refluxy as a way of dealing with too much food. You don't have to worry that she's not getting enough food as long as she's continuing to gain weight. You'll know that by your weigh-ins, which you write in her health record book.

Here's how you create a routine. You've been tracking when your baby's been eating and sleeping. Now you can see that your baby ate, fell asleep, and then woke up after a couple of hours and wanted to feed. That means she can go a couple of hours without a feed. She's grown, her tummy can hold more food at a time. In the beginning, it was probably only 2 ounces; now she can take 4 ounces or so and that will last her longer. So you take those two hours and stretch it out a bit—feed her at 2¼ hours, say, or 2½. Try a pacifier, to see if she will suck on that for a while.

What you want to end up doing is keep stretching out the time to go from on-demand to 2–4 hours, unless your baby is very refluxy, in which case you want do more frequent, small feedings.

Here's what it looks like:

FEEDING ROUTINE: 4–6 WEEKS

Here are two possible schedules so you can get the idea
of what a routine looks like. Time it either from
when your baby begins feeding or ends.

Time	Activity
SCHEDULE 1	
7:00 AM	breast-feed 20–40 minutes or bottle-feed 2–4 oz.
9:00 AM	same
11:00 AM	same
1:00 PM	same
3:00 PM	same
5:00 PM	same
7:00 PM	same
9:00 PM	same
11:00 PM	last feed, possible sleep through
4:00 AM	breast-feed 20–40 minutes or bottle-feed 2–4 oz.
SCHEDULE 2	
6:30 AM	breast-feed 20–40 minutes or bottle-feed 2–4 oz.
9:00 AM	same
11:00 AM	same
1:30 PM	same
3:30 PM	same
7:00 PM	same
9:30 PM	same
11:30 PM	same
4:00 AM	same
7:00 AM	same

As she gets older, she can take more milk at each feeding and therefore last longer. At 6–8 weeks, if bottle-feeding, add an extra ounce, and if it goes down, she should hold out for four hours as shown in the schedule below. Over the three months, bottle-feeders should go from eight bottles of 2–4 oz. at birth to six bottles of 4–5 oz. and then to five bottles of 5-6 oz.

If breast-feeding, you have to measure by time to gauge how much your baby is getting because you can't see what he's taking in. At 6–8 weeks, increase the time by ten minutes. As time goes on, increase again. Eventually, you'll start to recognize that your baby's intake will increase as he gets older. He's able to take in more faster and

---

FEEDING SCHEDULE: 6–8 WEEKS–3 MONTHS

Here you should be trying to progress through
these three phases over the six weeks.

6:30 AM	breast-feed 30–40 minutes or bottle-feed 4–5 oz.
9:30–10:00 AM	same
2:00 PM-ish	same
5:30 PM	same
9:00 PM	same
12:30 AM	same
6:00 AM	breast-feed 30–40 minutes or bottle-feed 5 oz.
10:30 AM	same
2:30–3:00 PM	breast-feed 30–40 minutes or bottle-feed 5 oz.
7:00 PM	same
11:00 PM	same
5:00–6:00 AM	breast-feed 20–30 minutes or bottle-feed 5–6 oz.
10:00 AM	same
2:30 PM	same
7:00 PM	same
11:30 PM	consider bottle-feeding here as it will be heavier in her tummy and will last longer

you'll be able to judge that he's had a proper intake of food in a shorter time. You'll feel the sense of emptiness, like "he's had a good feed." It's kind of like having a baby on a bottle who goes from a slow flow teat to a fast flow one. So you may sense that he's getting enough in twenty minutes where it used to be thirty or forty.

EXPECT DISRUPTIONS FOR ILLNESS

If your baby's sick—has a fever, or thrush, or some infection, it's important that she stay hydrated. But she may be off food, especially with thrush, which is painful. At these times, you need to recognize that the routine's all out the window, because your baby needs more frequent feedings so she stays hydrated and doesn't lose weight.

Teething and growth spurts also disrupt a routine. Or travel to other time zones. Both eating and sleeping can be affected. Do the best you can and reestablish as soon as possible.

PARENTCRAFT

In this section, you'll learn all the tricks of the parent trade: diaper changing, dressing, swaddling, bathing, trimming nails, taking temperatures, going out. With my techniques, you'll find that this is one of the easy parts.

0–3 Months

HOLDING AND CARRYING

Yes, your baby is a tiny, vulnerable being, but the good news is that she's a lot sturdier than you might have imagined. She's not made of glass. In fact, the more gently yet firmly you hold and carry them, the more secure they will feel and the happier they will be.

You probably already know that her neck needs to be supported. It's because her head is very big in comparison to the rest of her body, which makes it wobbly. Parents going for a kiss have been known to end up with a shiner if they're not careful.

A good basic holding and carrying position is with one hand supporting her head and neck, and the other her upper legs and bottom. Use it to pick her up or set her down, to carry her over one shoulder, to nurse or bottle-feed. That way she won't feel like she's falling, which may set off the startle reflex—a flailing of arms and legs that can startle both of you.

One of the key tasks of baby's first year is to strongly bond to his caregivers. It's the basis for his ability to bond later in life to loved ones of his own. Physical closeness, touching, cuddling—these are all ways to promote this crucial attachment. Closeness allows your baby to feel safe, and creates the intimacy that shows him he's loved and cared for. Holding and carrying helps create bonding as well as a sense of safety that will keep the crying down. A baby held is a baby content.

This usually isn't hard because all you want to do is cuddle her anyway! But because babies can't regulate their temperatures when they're first born, she may get very hot from your body heat. So be sure to put her down every now and again, for her sake as well as yours. My carrying recommendation doesn't mean you have to hold her 24-7. You've got things to do, if only going to the bathroom. It's better, for instance, for your baby to be where she can see you than be attached to your hip when you're trying to cook. That's dangerous!

When you have to lay your baby down, or sit your baby up, as much as possible keep her in eyeshot because she's very tiny. It makes her frightened if she doesn't know where you are. Give her something to distract herself with. Put one of those baby gyms over her seat or bassinet. She'll get used to seeing you from a distance and being able to play as well.

If you have to go from one room to the next, talk: "Hello, baby! It's okay. Mommy's coming back!" There's something very valuable in the fact that every time he doesn't see you and then he sees you, he learns you've come back. It's like peekaboo, isn't it? Eventually they understand that just because you're not in the room, it doesn't mean you're not there. And that helps him feel secure.

When it comes to holding and carrying, dads, grandparents, aunts—I'm talking to you too. For fathers: holding and carrying your baby is a chance to really connect. Perhaps the last time you held something with purpose was that football a few Sundays ago playing with your buddies in the park. Now you get to hold your baby and talk shop. For some dads, it's easy; for others, it's a little difficult at first as they feel so big in comparison and scared to hold their young one so new! But the more you practice, the more comfortable you'll become. Whether you're a big CEO or not, you're a star in your baby's life, and he needs all your love and care as well as Mom's.

A friend just had a baby boy. He couldn't wait to put him in the latest car seat, latest bouncer, latest stroller—he embraced all the equipment for his little one from the get-go. When I laughed about it, he replied, "Hey, he's a man's man and you know us dudes like gadgets! I'm starting him early!"

As your baby reaches three months, it will become easier to hold him as his neck muscles are stronger and he's bigger all over. You'll know how to maneuver around with a lot more ease, and your baby will be happy to be passed around as she is familiar with your touch, face, smell, and voice. All this discrimination allows him to be at ease in a loving environment. But be sure to watch for signs when your baby has had enough of being passed around like the latest edition of *People* magazine.

DIAPER CHANGING

To avoid diaper rash, change your baby as soon as he soils. Check inside the diaper frequently to make sure it's still dry. The cleaner and drier you keep his bottom, the less likely he is to develop a rash. This is especially important if you're bottle-feeding because that increases the possibility of rash. Be aware too when breast-feeding that different food you eat may cause diaper rash. So keep that bottom clean!

Whether you use cloth or paper diapers or the new combos, if you've never diapered a baby, you'll find it takes a bit of practice to get it properly onto a squirming, possibly wailing tiny bottom. Don't worry, you'll soon be an old pro. You can easily go through 8–10 diapers or more in the beginning. Here's the step-by-step:

- Make sure you have all supplies within reach before starting.
- Put your baby down on a clean changing mat.
- Remove dirty diaper. (If you have a boy, you may get sprayed as his penis is exposed to cold air. To minimize this you can quickly place a clean diaper on him as you remove the old.) Place dirty diaper out of reach so he won't accidentally fling his leg into poo. This will become more important as she gets older and more mobile.
- Clean bottom and genitals (front to back if you have a girl to avoid vaginal infections). Be sure to get in all the skin folds. When he's newborn, I like using warm water and cotton wool when you're at home. It's gentler on his delicate skin. Save the disposable wipes for when

you're out and make sure to buy the hypoallergenic ones. Constant use of wipes can cause diaper rash.

- Pat dry with his hand towel and make sure to dry in all those folds.
- If a rash appears, use a good diaper rash cream. Also, if he has a rash, make sure you give his bottom air time (time without a diaper on) and don't use any form of soap as it will sting.
- Lift up bottom, lay down clean diaper and fasten so that it's tight enough to keep from leaking but not so tight that it causes marks or discomfort. If you have a boy, make sure his penis is pointing down in the diaper so that he doesn't wet his undershirt. If the umbilical cord has not yet fallen off, make sure the diaper is below it.
- For extra leak protection, you may want a diaper cover.
- Put him in a safe spot and clean off changing pad with disinfecting spray. Put as much of the poo as possible down the toilet to keep the odor down when they are older, or use diaper genie to discard.
- If you're using cloth diapers and laundering them yourself, make sure you use a baby-friendly detergent. Never use fabric softener or anti-static sheets as they can irritate a baby's sensitive skin.

NEED TO KNOW

WHEN TO CALL THE DOCTOR

- The rash is on thighs, genitals, tummy instead of bottom (a sign of thrush).
- If your baby is six weeks or younger, or rash hasn't gone away within three days.
- She also has a fever, is eating poorly or losing weight.
- The rash is spreading to other parts of the body.
- In addition to redness, you see bumps, pimples, or open sores.

Notice I didn't mention using talcum powder. Research shows it can be dangerous to babies' lungs, so stay away. If you must, use cornstarch, which absorbs moisture. If you go that route, be sure to wash it off completely each time you change her, especially in skin folds, as it can breed bacteria. This is your choice, parents; I'm giving you the facts.

A final diaper word: whatever kind of diapers you're using, you may find you need to move up in size before the stated weight limit. The way you'll know is that she'll start leaking out the back.

PENIS CARE

If your boy has been circumcised, don't clean his penis for four days. Rather, coat a sterile pad with sterile petroleum jelly and place it on the tip after every diaper change to keep it from being irritated by the diaper. After day four, wipe the tip with wet cotton wool and pat dry with a cloth diaper. You may see yellow ooze or crust, or a few drops of blood. If it's oozing blood, call the doctor. If he's not urinating every six hours or so, call the doctor. You will know by the weight of his diaper. If you notice swelling, there could be an infection, so seek a doctor's advice.

If he's not circumcised, don't retract the foreskin to clean him. This can cause bleeding.

UMBILICAL CORD CARE

Your baby's cord will take 2–5 weeks to dry up and fall off. Until then, keep it dry and exposed to air as much as possible. Make sure the top of the diaper ends below the belly button. Fold down if need be. Be sure it's dry after a bath. Never pull it off, even if it's hanging by a thread. If you see oozing pus or redness on the skin around the belly button, consult your doctor.

DRESSING

When it comes to dressing your baby, look for clothes that are easy to get on and easy to get off. Take into consideration the textures and fabrics. Some babies have dermatitis or eczema, and so should be in all-cotton to allow the skin to breathe and not get irritated.

There are some babies who don't like being undressed and there are some babies that won't mind. If yours is one who cries, you're not doing anything wrong. She's just reacting to the change in temperature. She's cold. Place a blanket on top of her as soon as you take her clothes off and that should do the trick.

Your baby's head is the biggest part of her body when she's born. So to dress her in anything that goes over the head, gather up the cloth, stretch at the neckline with your fingers like you're playing cat's cradle, and put her head through first, and then the arms. It's no different than giving birth! Head first, then shoulders. Gather up long sleeves too, which will make it much easier to get her arms through. For sleepers, onesies, snap undershirts and other snap clothing, lay it out flat, place him on top of it, then put in arms and legs and snap.

Don't mess with shoes. They're actually bad for infant feet. Because babies' bones in their toes are soft, you need to make sure they aren't cramped or they won't grow properly. So don't put them in hard shoes until they're walking—and then only for when they go out. If what she's wearing doesn't cover her feet, put on soft booties or socks to keep those toes warm—and make sure there's plenty of room in there.

Since tiny babies can't regulate temperature well, my rule of thumb is to always put on one more layer than you're wearing. But don't over-bundle. Being too hot can also be problematic. If you're swaddling, remember to take that into account and dress her more lightly.

NAKED TIME

In order to help the umbilical cord dry and fall off, or to clear up diaper rash, let your newborn lie around naked as much as possible. Make sure he's not cold, especially in the winter.

Half of all newborns develop at least a mild case of jaundice after they come home. It's caused by babies being born with more red blood cells than they need. As the body gets rid of these, it produces a substance called *bilirubin*. Bilirubin must be absorbed by the liver, and if the liver can't do this quickly enough, the baby develops jaundice, which manifests as yellow cheeks and whites of the eyes. Five minutes in the late afternoon or early morning sun really helps to prevent this or clear it up—with a hat to protect her eyes, of course.

Be aware that there are two kinds of jaundice, one of which can be lethal. The dangerous kind usually develops within twenty-four hours of being born. If your baby is listless or becomes very yellow, see the doctor to make sure she doesn't have the serious kind. They now have incubators you can bring home if need be to clear up the common form of jaundice; call it your own baby spa!

BATHING

Until the umbilical cord dries up, give your baby a once-over with a warm sponge or cloth and mild liquid soap on his diaper changing mat. Make sure the bathroom is warm, and that there are no drafts or fans on him. Remove your watch and rings to prevent scratching tender skin. Wash his head last because it loses the most heat. Then wipe clean with a warm cloth and pat dry.

When it's time for a real bath, warm the bathroom and fill the baby bath with a couple inches of warm water. Test with your elbow. Hold her over the bath, supporting her neck with your thumb and your index finger of one hand. With the other hand, wash her head with mild, unscented liquid baby soap. Then place her in the bath, supporting her neck with your forearm, and cradle her body. (See diagram.) I would recommend bathing her every third day or so, depending on how dry her skin is. The more dry, the less frequent.

As with cleaning up when diapering, always clean girls' genitals front to back to avoid infection and no bubble baths or oils! They can irritate labias and vaginas. Pat dry, paying particular attention to the creases in legs and neck.

HEAD CARE

All babies are born with soft spots, or fontanels, on their skulls. They're there so that the head can grow at the rapid rate it does in the first few months. One is on top of the head in the front, which closes at between 9–12 months. The other is on top of the head in the back. It's smaller, and closes at around three months.

Even though we call them soft spots, they're really sturdy. Of course you want to be gentle with your baby's head, but despite what you may have been told, you don't have to be too afraid of these spots. You may see them pulsing and that's normal too. If it's seriously indented, that could be caused by dehydration, so make sure he's feeding enough. Check with the doctor if you're concerned.

You may also see thick yellow scales on your baby's head. That's cradle cap,

> **NEED TO KNOW**
>
> ### WARM WATER RELIEF
>
> A warm bath in the baby tub can be a good soothing aid for an infant who has a lot of gas or reflux, or is irritable. Place one arm under his neck and upper back, the other on his bottom and thighs and sway him through the water. It relaxes your baby just like it does for us adults soaking in a big tub.

EAU DE BABY

Know that amazing baby smell you love so much? It actually comes from a release of oil from your baby's head, which allows us to smell it and bond. From your baby's fontanel, "Baby Chanel."

which is harmless but unsightly skin that peels off. It will go away on its own, but you can speed it along by rubbing natural olive oil into his head and leaving it on for a few hours. Then give a slight circular massage on his head, and it will come off.

EAR CARE

Don't mess with the inside of your baby's ears. They're too sensitive. Far too sensitive. And never, never stick Q-tips in your baby's ear. They can puncture his eardrum and cause permanent hearing problems. That ear wax is not harmful in any way, except to your sensibilities. In fact, it actually helps keep out infection. So leave it be unless it's falling out of the outer ear. Then you can remove it. Do, however, clean the lobes and behind the ears.

EYE CARE

Some infants have a yellow crust or discharge in the corner of their eyes, which is caused by a blocked tear duct. Just wipe with cotton wool that you've wet with warm water. It should clear up in a few days. If it doesn't and the eye starts to swell underneath and when you lightly press on it with your little finger, it seems spongy, take her to the pediatrician, who will give you a saline solution to clear it up.

As babies get older, sometimes they can get sticky eye, or pinkeye, also known as *conjunctivitis.* You'll know when your child's got it because his eye is blood-shot, there's yellowing crust, and his eyelashes all stick together. It's highly con-tagious. See the doctor, and be very careful when cleaning her eye to wipe with a warm wet washcloth from the tear duct out. And then wash your hands and the cloth thoroughly.

BABY ACNE

Newborns often get acne, due to hormone changes from birth. It shows up usu-ally at the one-month mark. Just wash her face every day with water and it will disappear. It's more irritating to parents' vanity rather than for the baby.

Take note of what your baby's skin is like. Is it hot or cold, smooth or rough? You may find that your baby already has t-zones, meaning his face is slightly oilier in some places than others. The seasons do affect your baby's skin just like they do for adults. As your child gets older, in harsh winters you may want to coat a very small smear of Vaseline along their cheekbones for protection.

NAIL TRIMMING

Babies' fingernails and toenails can scratch their delicate skin and eyes, which can cause an abrasion of the cornea. That's why it's important to keep nails short.

When a baby is very tiny, up to a month, you can usually peel your baby's nails with your own fingernails—they're that soft. When you do this, be incredibly careful that you don't go too low. Otherwise you'll rip the undersurface as well.

Once the nails harden, then it's time for trimming. Here's how:

- Use baby nail clippers or safety scissors.
- Place her on your knee looking outward and then hold her hand and cut her nails as if you're cutting your own. It's much easier.
- Push down gently on the bottom of the nail with your finger. It will make the nail pop up a bit so it's easier to cut.
- Distract her by singing songs and talking about what you're doing. "Look at this little piggy . . ." That way she's paying attention to you rather than what you're doing and before you know it it's done.
- Make sure to cut all the nails straight so that you don't get any ingrown.
- You don't have to do all nails on both hands at once. If she's squirming too much, do a few and try again later.
- If you nip the skin, don't panic. Most every parent has. Just take a gauze pad or tissue and apply pressure until the bleeding stops. It will knit itself back together.

Nail trimming is all about confidence. The more you do it, the more comfortable you and your baby will be. If you're nervous, you'll make your baby nervous. I became the expert nail trimmer in my nanny years, and mothers used

SOCK TRICK

If at first you're too afraid to trim your baby's fingernails, just place a pair of cotton baby socks over her hands while she's sleeping. That way at least she won't scratch her face in her sleep. I prefer socks to mittens because they've got a little bit of elastic at the top and hold better at the wrist.

to bring their children around for a visit and a cut.

TAKING A TEMPERATURE

Taking a temperature is an important skill for parents because young babies can run really high fevers really fast. The best way to take a newborn's temperature is rectally. A normal rectal temperature is 100.4°F in kids under three.

- Make sure you have a rectal thermometer. If you're using a digital thermometer, mark it with an *R*. If you're using a glass one, learn to read the mercury line by rotating the thermometer slowly. It can be hard to see.
- Shake glass thermometer until it's below 98.6°, or turn on digital thermometer.
- Coat the tip with petroleum jelly.
- Put your baby on his back with his knees up to his tummy on a diaper (in case of accidents).
- Place slowly into your baby's rectum about 1 inch, and then squeeze his buttocks together. With a glass thermometer, wait three minutes. With digital, wait till it beeps.

Call the doctor if his temperature is higher than 100.4°F if he's under three months; 101°F if he's between 3–6 months; 103° if he's six months or older. In the meantime, you can make him more comfortable by stripping him down to a T-shirt. Make sure he gets plenty of fluids—breast or bottle. You can also give a tepid bath and allow to air-dry. If that doesn't bring it down, go to the hospital.

If you are seeing a temperature that's higher than 104° in the first three months, don't hesitate, take him straight to the hospital. It's as simple as that. That high a fever can cause serious dehydration and be dangerous.

See the back of this book for a description of common ailments in the first year, as well as an emergency first aid guide.

FEBRILE SEIZURES OR CONVULSIONS

Some infants have convulsions when their fever shoots up. They usually aren't dangerous, unless caused by meningitis, but can be incredibly scary for the parent who is unaware of the possibility. They usually don't begin until babies are about nine months, but can start before. The baby convulses, eyes rolled back in his head, usually for about two minutes but it can be up to ten.

If this happens to your baby, place him down where he can't hit his head on anything and time the convulsions. Call the ambulance or doctor while timing. Have your baby checked. Something is causing the fever spike.

MASSAGE

Want to help your baby's digestion, circulation, sleep, growth, lower her stress and yours, and increase bonding between you? Try infant massage. You don't need formal training. Here's all you need to know:

- Do it when your baby is calm, like after a feeding bath, or nap.
- Heat the room to 75°F or higher.
- Remove all jewelry and your watch. Have fingernails short.
- Put down the changing pad and place a soft towel on top of it.
- Remove your baby's clothes and lay him on a towel or in his diaper.
- Wash your hands in warm water to heat them.
- Rub a bit of baby oil, cream, or gel in your hands.

ADMINISTERING MEDICINE

If the doctor prescribes medicine, measure carefully and try this method to get it all in:

- Fill dropper or syringe.
- Take your finger and pull out a corner of her cheek to make a pocket.
- Drop the medicine in one drop at a time into the pocket until it's all gone.
- If she hates the taste, try refrigerating it first. Cold medicine tastes less strong. Or ask the doctor if it comes in any other flavor.
- Slightly tilting her head back will help her swallow when older.

- Massage your baby with your fingertips using a light touch. Do not massage his face with oil.
- Arms: rub up and down gently one at a time with a stroking motion. Legs: squeeze lightly and knead each. Tummy: rub one palm in a circle. Back: place one hand on each side of his spine and move one up while the other goes down and then reverse. Chest: make a heart-shaped motion with your fingertips. Feet: use your two thumbs, one thumb on ball and one on heel. Stroke upward.
- Spend no more than 10–15 minutes.

OUT AND ABOUT

Doctors often recommend not taking babies under three months too far because their immune systems have not fully developed and they haven't had all their injections. But babies love to be taken out in a stroller, and I don't see any harm in taking a healthy walk in the park or meeting a friend for lunch occasionally. It's important for you to be able to get some fresh air and also to meet up with some friends if you're feeling up to it, so why not? It's not as if you're going to be highly active or doing this every day or taking him out in a rainstorm. Use your good judgment. Of course if you or your baby or friend is sick, then home it is!

Strollers should be used from six months on, as the backs are not supportive enough till then. Car seat carriers on wheels or strollers with lie-flat positions are best for 0–6 months.

It's actually easier to take newborns out than once your baby gets mobile. All you need is your equipped diaper bag from Chapter 3, a bottle of formula unless you're breast-feeding, an infant seat or stroller, and you're ready to go. Strap her into that rear-facing infant car seat in your car's backseat and when you reach your destination, place her in the infant seat or use her car seat, and take her with you. If you're lucky, she'll fall asleep during the drive and won't wake up till after you're finished doing what it is you're up to. Just be prepared to leave if she starts crying and won't be comforted.

You can also take her to the grocery store—clip the car seat into the grocery cart or use the ones with the built-in seats (after cleaning with a baby wipe). For longer trips, bring a change of clothes for yourself as well as her in case of emergencies, and be sure to pack enough formula if bottle-feeding.

STIMULATION AND EXPLORATIONS

You know about the importance of taking care of your baby's physical needs. Now it's time to focus on her mental and emotional ones. Stimulating your baby's brain is key to intellectual development and mental health. Her brain is very active, twice as active as an adult's. Researchers estimate that 50 percent of the human's brain development occurs in the first six months of life, and 70 percent is complete by the end of the first year. That's an awful large amount. That's why it's especially important to interact with your baby throughout the first year.

This is not all about giving him fancy educational toys. Science is now learning that babies' brains actually get formed up by their interactions with people and explorations in their environment. It's like an electrical circuit, all potentiality, waiting for you to flip the switch on through interaction and stimulation. So the best things you can do are cuddle and interact with him as much as possible when he's awake, encouraging him to reach his healthy developmental milestones that you learned about in the developmental overview.

Here are some of the crucial abilities you'll be helping stimulate:

- Auditory development: hearing and speaking.
- Visual development: seeing at close and far range, as well as visual tracking; the ability to follow something with the eyes and visual memory; the ability to recall faces, images, and objects, which are crucial to be able to read.
- Balance: the ability to maintain body positions against the force of gravity.
- Eye-foot coordination: gauging distance and depth with the eyes and processing that information to coordinate movement.
- Eye-hand coordination: directing the position and the motion of the hands in response to visual information to grasp things.
- Fine motor skills: the ability to use hands to pick up small objects and handle things like spoons.
- Gross motor skills: the ability to move the whole body in a coordinated way.

- Object permanence: the concept that an object or a person exists even if you can't see them.
- Trust: knowing that one's basic needs will be cared for.

Remember, as I said in the developmental overview, babies move at different paces and some achieve skills quicker than others. It's important to notice when she's achieved a milestone so that you can encourage her to do the next thing and not wait because she's not a certain age. For example, as soon as you see your baby gaining more control over her arms, hands, and wrists, then it's time to encourage more fine motor development. So you may end up reading ahead to find out things you can do next, based on your child's development.

In the resource guide, I've provided a list of the toys your baby can enjoy over the year so you can know all the good options. I have not put them in age stages because each baby is unique. When purchasing, take note of the recommended ages on the packaging to get an idea. But be aware that it may not be appropriate for your child. There's nothing worse than buying something beyond his level of development. It will cause frustration for your baby and you.

Even with the best intentions, you can end up with things that she won't be able to use yet. For instance, someone might buy her a little wooden tricycle that you know she can't ride. However, you can put her on top of it and then hold her and push it. But of course things that are just too advanced need to be put aside until she can really enjoy them.

Likewise, don't hang onto toys that he's developed past. I've gone into many homes recently where toddlers are still playing with baby toys. You want to stay one step ahead and add things that will challenge her. Bag up the newborn toys once she's passed that stage and save for the next baby. Or give to charity, a friend, or relative.

Don't plop him in front of the television. TV or DVDs don't provide the kind of interaction a baby needs and can cause obesity later due to lack of movement. If you're desperate for a break, a few minutes won't hurt, but it shouldn't be a regular thing.

There is an isolation that speaks volumes when a child has not been given human interaction. The more you put in in the early years, the greater the payoff down the line. When I walk into a house, I can see where there's been no stimulation, because the child is not where he might be if given the time and interaction. This affects his developmental stages, emotional development, and intellect. Stimulation takes time; fortunately, most parents find it a lot of fun too.

When playing, watch for signs of tiredness: turning away, getting irritable. A baby doesn't have a long attention span, and will soon make it obvious that he's had enough. Read your baby's cues. Sometimes it's not the right time—like when he's just been fed and has gas. This is a process of trial and error. You may try something and your baby doesn't respond and you think, "Oh, I won't do that again." And you try something else.

Be realistic as well. You're not an amusement park. You don't have to fill every minute of the day or give your child one long roller coaster ride. You've got other things to take care of. You want to give short spurts of stimulation, which will allow you to feel content as a parent, and your baby to feel content with the time she's spent with you.

Also, a big part of healthy stimulation is creating experiences for others within your trusted circle to connect with your baby. The task shouldn't all fall on you.

Classes

Baby activity classes are lovely because they offer more human interaction. Parents ask me when's a good time to start, and I say it's entirely up to you. If you're wondering what a good age is for a particular activity, most have a starting age listed. In addition to paid classes, places of worship have playgroups and coffee mornings, and there are also organized activities at workplaces. Check around.

A Playful Attitude

It's important not to make this a chore. As much as we want our babies to reach those milestones, it's not about ticking it off: "Okay, right, today I've worked on his visual stimulation and yesterday I worked on his audio." It should feel very organic because play comes naturally to babies. So it's important that you feel the same way, even if it's a bit awkward in the beginning. Some parents have never been around babies and all of a sudden there he is and you think, "Right, what do I do?" Have fun!

Babies aren't born knowing the world is a wonderful place. You are their teacher. You are showing them how beautiful the world is, how much fun it is. You're actually building those memories in everything that you do. So it's very inspiring because you create your baby's world for him, and that's why it's even more important that you play together.

I was told recently by one father that too much information makes parents feel overloaded and afraid. This book is really about going back to basics, and so in this section you'll find very simple things you can do with little or no equipment. What follows are suggestions to get you started at each age stage.

PLAY IDEAS

When your baby is first born, the most important thing is to have lots of face-to-face time. Lots of hugs, lots of kisses, talking in that high-pitched, lovely, warm voice, calling her name. Eventually she'll respond with a head turn, a gurgle, a smile. Being in front of a tiny baby brings out the mush in most of us. But if it doesn't, don't worry about it. Just start off doing something.

Everything is new for your baby. Don't be surprised if you become overly enthusiastic and you give your baby such a very large and noisy kiss or jiggle that she cries. Some newborns take sudden noises or movements with a grain of salt and they won't move at all; others will be quite frightened by them. You're learning as much as your baby right now. I like to play around with my voice and make different noises as well as sing different lullabies to find his preferences.

Equally important is just to allow your baby to be. Particularly for the first four weeks, he's going to be sleeping an awful lot. So it's important to find that balance where you're stimulating your baby and having still time with him on your lap and gazing into his eyes and talking softly. The sound of your voice and the feel of your hands are very reassuring.

A lot in this year is about prepping for future development. In the beginning, babies can only see in black and white, but they still have colored objects. We know they're not going to read at one year old, but we still read them stories. They don't get it now, but doing it now helps them get it later.

SENSORY STIMULATION
Stimulate their sense of touch, sound, and sight. Gently shake a variety of little rattles so she hears different things. Place her on her little mats and scrunch up

pieces of paper for new sounds. Take a makeup brush or feather and stroke her arms, legs, and face. How does she respond?

Even though babies are fascinated by sounds and voices because they can hear in the womb, they're not able to locate where the sound has come from. So one thing you can do is to rattle or make a noisy toy move from left to right in front of your baby so that he can start to establish where the noise is coming from. Once he recognizes sounds in front of him, make the sound on the side and see if he turns his head.

Even though as a newborn her vision is blurry, that doesn't mean that you can't have objects within a close range to look at. Put objects by the bouncer seat as well as having a mobile overhead. You'll know when she's starting to focus because she'll aim toward something with a hand. That's when you can start putting objects above her so she learns she can lift her eyes on her head and also move her head to see. You're helping her develop her vision tracking. This is also when it's good to hang a pretty thing at the back of her rear-facing car seat. It should be short enough so she can bat at it but not be able to get tangled in it.

TALK IT UP

Stimulate your child with lots of talk. Baby talk is fine, but intersperse it with adult words too so you challenge his language development. Babies who are spoken to are more assertive and learn language faster. I always tell parents to be animated because babies absolutely love it.

For some parents it's really difficult to start talking. There you are staring at your baby, thinking "What am I going to say?" Just say what you see: "You've got lovely big eyes. Oh, and what a teeny little chin . . ." You can say almost anything, as long as it's not a rant about your terrible day.

Another easy way to start is to pick up your baby and show her herself in a mirror: "Who's this, who's this?" For now she won't know, but the time will come when she coos and smiles and really shows interest in what you're saying. Remember, the more opportunities you give her to practice these skills, the sooner they develop.

LET YOUR INNER POP STAR OUT

One key skill as a parent is to learn to be comfortable singing! Children love music. In the beginning, sing lullabies. Don't know any? Why should you? Go out and buy the CD and get the nursery rhyme book while you're at it. Or be your own Elton John and make up lyrics.

Humming is fabulous too because it creates a soothing vibration, for you and your baby. Hum or sing when bathing, feeding, dressing, driving, etc. and you'll find those tasks are easier on both of you.

TUMMY TIME

Since she must sleep on her back for safety, as she reaches the two-month mark or so, be sure to give her "tummy time" when she's awake to help physical development—babies can raise their heads on their stomachs more easily at first than on their backs. But her neck muscles must be strong enough before you do this, or she'll just end up facedown on the mat.

Partly why I'm against holding babies all day is that it's good for them to be lying down on the floor, on their backs at first, with you beside them, tickling and touching them. Then they see you and interact with you while having their own space. So get down on the floor and put props in front of your child's face to stimulate his visual ability. Hold objects at about 8–15 inches away so they can see them well. Help your baby gain eye-hand coordination by moving objects in front of or above him that he can bat at.

"PLAY IT AGAIN, SAM"

Repetition is incredibly important. Sing the same songs, recite the same nursery rhymes, and rattle the same rattle over and over. These repetitions will make her smile, turn around, and gurgle. She's recognizing the pattern, which causes great delight. Eventually, she'll remember and do back what she's been taught.

CHANGE OF SCENERY

Take your baby with you from room to room and out and about. He'll love the stimulation of new sights, sounds, and smells. Introduce him to other children and adults, one at a time if you have a shy, sensitive child. Believe it or not, even babies this young get bored!

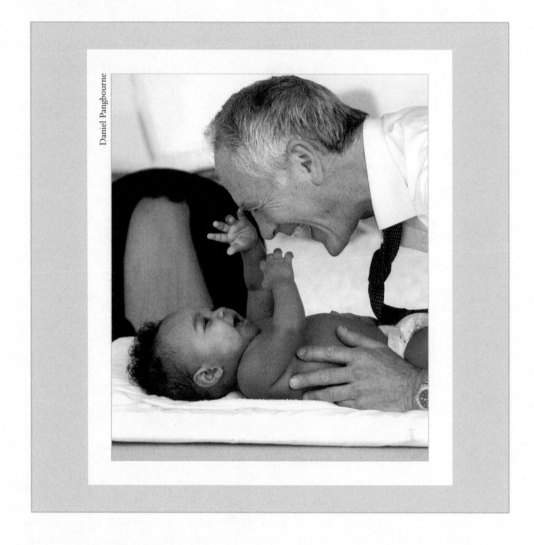

Daniel Pangbourne

CHAPTER 5

Three to Six Months

PARENTS' JOURNEY

Congratulations! You've come a long way in a short time. Things are getting easier, aren't they? Good for you! You've paid attention to your baby and are starting to be able to see patterns in what various cries mean, and when she eats and sleeps. You can read her better and so have more calm moments. You've just spent three months together, and know her likes and dislikes, her favorite rattle, her preferred burping position.

You're becoming more in sync, in tune, which allows you to be one step ahead of your baby. Rather than just respond to her needs, you start to anticipate them. You're halfway between the parent who *wants* to know everything and the one who *does* know everything about your baby!

By now, his temperament is showing itself. I've seen lots of parents make jokes about that: "Oh yeah, he likes his food, just like your side of the family!" You're finding your humor back again, aren't you? In the very beginning, everything is very serious as you want to get it *right*. Now you've earned your badge, so you can begin to have more fun. Plus, he's getting more active, so the process of baby care may be more enjoyable for you. With all the smiles and the laughs, you get feedback that you're on the right track. Hopefully you're finding it easier to give your baby what he needs.

As much as you're recognizing what your baby needs, the two of you are recognizing what you need, as well. You know when you need some time for yourself and how to balance baby care with the rest of your life. Hopefully you're not as tired. You've got some kind of acceptable house management going on, and your emotions aren't so much on the surface. You remember feeling exhausted or overwhelmed, but the feelings themselves are (hopefully) gone. Your feet have definitely touched the ground.

You've also learned from your mistakes: I went to the park and didn't even bring any wipes with me. Those mistakes have also taught you to be adaptable—you know you can figure out what to do even when you don't have the proper equipment. Your competence and confidence are growing. Because you did it from 0–3 months, you know that you can do it from 3–6 months, right?

This stage is about creating lots of opportunities to stimulate your baby's development. This is the time to get out more into the world together—to join Mommy & Me–type classes, which are as much for you to bond with other moms as it is for the baby's sake. You may find yourselves starting to seek out more resources and more connection to other parents going through the same stage. It helps to recognize that you're not alone: "Oh, hey! Our baby has the same cold that Johnny down the road has." And, "I'm not the only one who's not up for sex every night."

You open up into a world where you recognize very quickly that the more you know, the more you want to seek and find even more resources. You want more information because you recognize that you have more choices now. And that's very empowering between the third and the sixth month. You *want* to be the best. You wanted to be the best in the beginning, but now you're secure enough to recognize quite comfortably that you don't know it all. Embrace your exploration because it will lead you to become even more confident.

One of the greatest things about having a baby is that you continue to love every day. Your love just grows and grows and grows and grows. That's because you've spent more and more time together. And it's only the beginning of that wonderful connection.

DEVELOPMENTAL OVERVIEW

Physical

She'll continue to gain 1½–2 pounds a month on average. But how much she weighs and how long she is is less important than the fact that she is growing. Every baby has her own growth rate, which your doctor will track. As long as she's consistently growing at the same rate, there's no need for alarm. Talk to the doctor if you have concerns.

She'll be awake more during the day, and since her stomach is larger, she will probably not need the middle of the night feeding. As a result, by four months, she—and you—will be sleeping seven to eight hours at a go. How lovely! If that's not happening, she may need more stimulation in the evening or more food just before going down for the night.

This time is all about beginning to move, which he will learn in stages as his head and neck muscles and sense of balance develop. First, he'll hold up his head and shoulders when placed on his tummy. Then, at around five months, he'll do a baby push-up. You'll see him "swimming" on his tummy too, kicking legs and waving arms with head up. It will be easy to pull him into a stand.

At some point he'll roll over, usually from front to back first. This often happens "out of the blue," which is why you should never leave a baby unattended on any high surface. In the beginning, once he's rolled onto his back, he's stranded because his muscles aren't strong enough to flip him back onto his tummy. By six months, however, he'll be doing it like a pro and will begin to pull himself across the floor on his tummy, the first step to crawling. At the six-month mark, he'll also be able to sit up unassisted, and can stand when you hold him up.

By month four, her little hands will put things in her mouth, so beware what you leave within her grasp. She'll grab her toes and they might go in the mouth too. She doesn't know how to use her thumb though (that doesn't kick in until about nine months). So she'll be clumsy. Larger objects are easier than small, and you may find she grips tightly onto things, including your hair or clothes.

She'll start to explore other parts of her body too, such as her genitals, while being changed. Put something just out of reach and she'll struggle to get to it. She'll begin splashing in the bath and put everything in her mouth.

By this time, she'll be imitating sounds you make and will be able to hear

ntinues to develop, and she'll likely prefer objects
actually tell the difference now between a real face

'll probably get his first tooth. But there is tremen-
me babies are even born with a tooth; others don't
birthday.

t four months your baby will start to respond to you
be picked up. That's such a precious moment. So is
her first laugh—which typically occurs in the fifth month. You'll find yourself
doing all kinds of things to hear that wonderful giggle.

Around this time, he'll discover cause and effect—the rattle makes a noise
when I shake it. And Mommy and Daddy also react when I drop something on
the ground! He'll begin to drop things on purpose to get a response from you.
He's experimenting with his environment and learning object constancy. You
may also see signs that he has memory of people and routines, and he may become attached to a particular toy. He'll look forward to feeding as a social time,
beyond just nourishment.

At five months, he may exhibit signs of jealousy if you hold other babies and
will begin to be wary of strangers, although may not yet have full-blown stranger
anxiety. This is when he also starts to demonstrate his preferences—turning his
head if he's not hungry and expressing frustration at not being able to do something he wants. You'll begin to hear sounds that indicate emotions: fear, anger,
dislike. That angry cry sounds different from the tired or hungry one.

By month six, he will begin to imitate your emotions and actions. Try it—
smile and see what he does. Now frown. Bang a toy. Sneeze. You'll be amazed at
what a mimic he is. He'll start imitating sounds in combinations (da, da, da) and
watch your mouth closely when you speak. You may see him respond to music
too, by bouncing, humming or swaying.

Is she easygoing or headstrong? Calm or rambunctious? Shy or outgoing? These
inborn tendencies will emerge even more strongly now. There's not a lot you can
do to change your baby's temperament. It's up to you to adapt with more routine
and calm in the case of the highly strung child; more quiet attention and time to

warm up to a new situation for the shy one; more physical stimulation for the rambunctious one. It's your job to pay attention to who this little one is and what she needs, and then provide that to the best of your ability.

BABYPROOFING

Before your baby gets mobile, it's time to make sure you've got all hazards out of reach: pesticides, detergents, alcohol, bleach, plant fertilizer, houseplants (many are poisonous if eaten), medicines—anything that she can put into her mouth that can harm her should be stored up high or in locked cupboards. Ditto for sharp objects: knives, scissors, etc.

WHEN TO CALL THE DOCTOR

- Refuses to cuddle by four months
- Doesn't smile by five months
- Shows no affection for the primary care-taker
- Can't sit with help by six or seven months
- Doesn't respond to sounds
- Doesn't laugh by six months

COMMON POISONOUS PLANTS

Some of these are more deadly than others, and this is not a complete list. Best to get all plants out of harm's way, especially as some children are allergic to pollen.

- poinsettias, holly berries, and mistletoe
- dieffenbachia
- poison ivy
- hydrangeas
- Swedish ivy
- some philodendrons
- lily of the valley
- English ivy
- rhododendrons and azaleas

- oleander
- foxglove
- larkspur
- hyacinth, daffodil, and narcissus bulbs
- laurel
- yew
- deadly nightshade
- elephant's ear
- sweet peas

There are plenty of safety gadgets that can be bought. Make sure you take the time to do this! These things can be complicated. But half an hour of putting that lock on the door could very well save your child's life. Because one minute he isn't even able to crawl and the next, he's in the cupboard pulling everything out and putting it in his mouth.

Make sure you check every room. I've seen families put a lock on the kitchen cleaning supplies and forget they keep their bathroom cleaning stuff in cupboards that can easily pull open.

Store all medicines and liquids in their original containers so you can tell what they are and what to do in case of ingestion. Throw old medicines away into a container that can't be opened.

Now's also the time to cover all plug sockets so he can't stick his tiny finger in there, and put window guards on all windows your child could get to. Put bulbs in any empty light sockets. Get cable ties to cover the wires for your TV, DVD player, etc.

Make sure humidifiers, portable heaters, etc. are beyond his reach when he's in his crib.

Bags can suffocate. Get rid of plastic dry cleaning and shopping bags immediately. If you save them to use again, get a bag dispenser and hang it up high somewhere out of reach.

Scan Daily

By six months, anything within reach will get scooped up and popped in his mouth. So be sure that all toys he can get to have no small parts that can break off (like older brother's car wheels, for instance). Keep older children's toys from the baby's. Ditto pet toys and pet food.

Whenever you put him down, scout around to make sure there are no small items that he can choke on. Also make sure there's nothing between the sofa cushions. When there's a baby around, I become like a metal detector, *bip-bip-bip-bip!* I find all kinds of things. For instance, Dad's rushed in the morning and he has his shirt dry-cleaned and it has *pins* in it. And I find a pin on the floor! So be sure to scan, scan, scan every day.

Small round items are extreme choking hazards because babies' airways are small and their muscles aren't well developed so they have more trouble swallowing than adults. That's also why when you begin to serve solid food, at around four months, it should be pureed. And never leave him alone when eating. More on this later.

If you're in doubt if something is a choking hazard, you can buy a choke tube or small-parts tester. Or use a toilet paper roll tube. If it can fit inside, it's too small.

Make sure the high chair is not by a

COMMON CHOKING HAZARDS

NEED TO KNOW

■ Coins, buttons, beads, marbles, rings, earrings, pins, pen and marker caps, thumbtacks, paper clips, foam balls that compress, toy car wheels, plastic eyeballs from teddies and dolls, button-sized batteries, bottle caps, balloons

window or any appliances and make sure you keep all hot liquids—coffee, tea, soup—out of reach. Absolutely, positively strap your child in the high chair! My word! The number of parents who do not put the harness on because he cries at being strapped in! Here's one of your first chances as a parent to do what's right, regardless of whether he likes it or not. He'll get used to it.

Make sure your junk drawer is locked or in a spot she can't get to.

Toys should not have dangling strings (cut them off) or batteries unless they are in a child-safe compartment (able to be opened only with a screwdriver). If a toy breaks and has sharp edges, get rid of it. Ditto any with small parts that could break off. Toy boxes should have safety hinges and ventilation holes. Don't let your baby chew on books or other printed material. It can be toxic.

Do a general wipe-down every day of his toys, because babies spit, dribble, and bring up their food. Then they put their toys in their mouths. Wash what you can wash if they're cloth toys and wipe over the rest.

Be sure that any home he spends time in—child minder's, Grandma's, etc.— has also been babyproofed, and pay extra attention when friends and relatives come to visit. Be sure that bags are placed up high. Don't leave him alone outside, even for a minute.

Sun Protection Is Crucial!

I feel very strongly about protecting your baby from the sun. I see too many parents being irresponsible about this. I've seen too many babies with bright red cheeks cavorting in the water with parents doing nothing. This is not something to take lightly. Sun protection is your moral responsibility. Research shows that even *one* serious sunburn as a child predisposes you to skin cancer as an adult.

Use hypoallergenic baby sunscreen (SPF 30 or higher) on all exposed skin, and put it on at least fifteen minutes before going out. Find the one that works best for your baby; some can give a rash to babies with sensitive skin. And that thing about sunscreen being waterproof? Reapply frequently, especially if she's gotten wet.

Always make sure you put a T-shirt on her even when she's in the water. Put it on after you've applied the sunscreen. And don't forget a hat, even in the water! Keep them in the shade as much as possible in warm weather. No matter how much sunscreen you used, if she's turning pink, she's burned, so get her inside!

Also, lead by example yourself. No good saying when she's fifteen months, "Come on, put this on," when she's never seen you do it yourself.

SETTING FIRM GROUND

Routines

You have a history now to fall back. You can look back and see the good that's been happening, and think, "Oh, that works! That's what I'm going to do now because that worked yesterday." As you create more of a routine, understand that babies are sometimes unpredictable. Things may work on Wednesday and not on Friday. You've got to have a certain amount of patience. You can't just try something once and if it doesn't work, give up. And remember, all kinds of things can disrupt your routine. It's your job to flex around those and then reestablish. It's about creating cornerstones of a routine to fill in gaps.

According to the National Sleep Foundation, between 3–11 months, your baby should be sleeping 9–12 hours a night plus having 1–4 naps a day of thirty minutes to two hours, for a total of 12–15 hours. I wholeheartedly agree. Here's my suggested routine for this age period. I'm showing you a starting point at three months and an ending schedule at six. Over the three months, you will be gradually adjusting to end up at the six month schedule.

SLEEP ROUTINE: 3–6 MONTHS	
Age	*Activity*
3 months	play
	mid-morning nap (2 hours)
	play
	nap (2 hours)
	play
	afternoon catnap (30 minutes)
	bedtime
6 months	play
	mid-morning nap (1 hour)
	play
	afternoon nap (2 hours)
	play (30–40 minutes)
	bedtime

Sleeping Through the Night

If you've introduced solids and have a consistent meal plan going (see Feeding Routine on pages 130–31), at five or six months you can create for a proper bedtime routine, which means you put her to sleep at 10:00 and she consistently doesn't wake up till morning. First, establish a nice little bedtime routine of about twenty minutes: perhaps a massage, rocking, then a lullaby, and off to bed. The idea is to get her drowsy, not asleep so she can learn to go to sleep on her own. In the 6–9 months section, you'll learn the Controlled Crying technique to get them to sleep through the night, but I would not try this before six months.

Between 4–6 months, you have the choice to put your baby in his own room if you have the option. Start by placing the bassinet into the crib so that he'll feel secure. A wide space straightaway can make him feel rather insecure

I swear by baby sleep sacks, since so many times babies wake up because they've become too cold as their temperature drops when they're sleeping. Also they help prevent overheating as they come in a variety of breathable fabrics.

with so much space around him. Then after a couple of days, place your baby down for his naps directly in the crib and then, when he's fine with that, in the evening.

You can also buy angel wings that are like tiny bolsters. You place the baby in the middle when she's lying on her back and the bolsters keep her snug in the middle to help her feel more secure. You can also create the same effect by tightly rolling up two blankets and placing them on either side of her to keep her from rolling over.

Put that little baby mobile on or that little teddy that pulls down and makes a sweet lullaby. The ritual will become very pleasant as she begins to understand that when she goes into the crib and that little music is played, it's time for sleep. You're going to have a lot more alert and astute baby at six months so it is important to make sure that any mobile that's hanging over the crib is not too low, so that your baby can't do any harm to herself with ribbons or cords if she grabs hold of it and pulls it down.

Once a baby is six months old, I'm not against them holding onto a favorite blankie or stuffed animal that smells of themselves to go to sleep, for years and years. I even know some parents now who've still got their blankies as a keepsake.

Sometimes babies get turned around and think day is night and night is day. To get him back on a normal schedule, make sure it's really bright in the morning and dark in the evening. Keep him as active and stimulated in the day as possible, and as quiet and placid in the evening. He'll get with the program.

Crying

By now you're probably much better at figuring out why your baby is crying. One reason to really pay attention now is her need for stimulation. Babies often cry from boredom.

MAKING SLEEPING EASIER

There are things you can do to help him go to sleep easily and stay asleep:

- Make sure he's getting enough milk and solids in the day.
- Get outside in fresh air. Babies who are given walks in strollers really do sleep better at night.
- Avoid him getting overtired; it actually interferes with babies' ability to fall asleep. So get a nap routine going.
- Make sure his diaper is dry.
- Give him lots of exercise and stimulation during the day. Do the stimulations I suggest for this age range.

When you have something to do, put him in a bouncy seat where he can sit properly and watch you, which allows him to be stimulated visually and auditorially without having to be held. If he continues to cry, do what you're going to do and then go up to him and offer reassurance with hugs and kisses. Pick him up, give him cuddles, and then put him back down again. Then go back to what you were doing and say, "Mommy's here, look, Mommy's here. Look what I'm doing." Eventually his crying will become sporadic, then he will stop and take note to look and listen.

Praise

Whenever your baby does something right, let her know. Praise for feeding, for taking a good nap, for playing, for sitting in the car seat. Verbal praise creates encouragement and helps development. Your little one is never too young for praise!

FEEDING

As your baby grows, it will take less time to feed him, as you and he get the hang of it. However, the older he gets, the more he will look around and be curious. Try to keep him focused by creating a calm, quiet feeding environment. Otherwise you'll find he's not feeding enough, only to get hungry an hour later.

Somewhere between 4–6 months, it's time to add solid foods to your baby's diet. You'll know when it's the right time because her weight gain may have stalled and she's hungrier and hungrier. Plus she'll show interest in your food.

The good news about adding solid foods is that she'll more be more likely to sleep through the night because her tummy will be full. In the beginning though, the majority of her nourishment will still come from milk or formula.

Food should be introduced gradually, a few spoonfuls at a particular mealtime. Only give one type of food at a time so you can judge whether something creates a bad reaction or if she doesn't like it. Start with baby cereal (rice cereal is great because it is rarely allergic) mixed with formula, breast milk or cooled, boiled water. Put a tiny bit on a baby spoon or your finger to begin with.

Expect a look of uncertainty when he first tastes solids. The flavor and texture is very different from milk. If he spits it out, it doesn't necessarily mean he doesn't like it. It might be that he's trying to figure out what to do. If he refuses altogether, wait a week or try another food. A couple spoonfuls in the beginning are just fine. When he turns his head away, that's a sign he's full or doesn't like it. Don't force it. Also, be aware that babies at 4–6 months poke their tongue in and out to make saliva to water down the food before swallowing it, so don't view that as a sign of rejection.

At first, feeding will be very messy. Make sure you use a big bib and have my fave, a clean cloth diaper on your shoulder. Put a plastic mat or towel under the high chair or infant seat if you are really worried. Use a plastic spoon. She may roll the food around a lot, exploring the experience of eating. Lots may land on the floor or bib. Eventually she'll get the hang of it. You want to work up to a dozen spoonfuls or so at a meal.

Once cereal's well tolerated, I like to make my own homemade, organic baby foods. It's incredibly easy. Begin with organic root vegetables: carrots, sweet potatoes. Wash well, peel, steam until soft, puree in the blender, pour into ice cube trays, and freeze. When it's time for a meal, pop one or two out into a dish, warm in the microwave, stir to get rid of any hot spots, test on your wrist or use one of those temperature tester spoons that turn a different color if the food is too hot. Then do organic fruits: apple and pear sauce, mashed bananas, then other organic vegetables like peas, zucchini, string beans, and avocados last because they have light skins, then pureed white meats like chicken and turkey breast, then finally red meats. For meats, cook in milk or steam, then put in the blender. I love my steamer and blender. With them, I'm on a roll of food-making heaven.

I love the simplicity of you being able to give your baby what she needs nutritionally through all the wonderful vitamins in these all-natural purees. Make sure all food is thoroughly cooked and pureed to avoid choking, and if she seems to be having an allergic reaction, get to the hospital or doctor right away. The more variety she's exposed to when young tends to result in a less picky eater when older.

Serve diluted baby juices or cooled boiled water along with food to avoid problems with constipation, which often is the result of the introduction of solids. The natural sugar in juice can cause bowel movements.

If you use store-bought baby food, stay away from those that contain the words *corn syrup, fructose, dextrose,* or any word ending in *—ose* or any artificial flavors or colors. Those are all added sugars. Don't feed your baby from the jar. Spoon food into a dish first to avoid bacterial contamination from saliva. If you feed from a jar,

NEED TO KNOW

ALLERGY SIGNS

- rashes or hives
- gas, diarrhea, excessive reflux, stomach cramp
- stuffy or runny nose
- wheezing
- swollen eyelids, lips, or throat
- irritability
- vomiting/choking, coughing, overproduction of saliva

throw away any leftover portion. Refrigerate any open jars and use within two days or throw away. If you use food from a can, run the can opener through the dishwasher before using and wash the lid before opening. Never store any unused portion in the can. Store food in plastic or glass containers only. Bacteria breeds quickly if food is not stored properly.

FEEDING SCHEDULE FOR INTRODUCING SOLIDS

In some age frames, I've given two schedules. That means the first is for when your baby is younger, transitioning over the three months to the second schedule.

Time	Activity
4–6 MONTHS	
Morning	bottle or breast-feed
Noon	lunch: solids
Night	bottle or breast-feed
4–6 MONTHS	
Morning	breakfast: solids
Noon	lunch
Night	bottle or breast-feed
6–9 MONTHS	
Morning	breakfast
Noon	lunch
Night	dinner: solids
9–12 MONTHS	
Morning	breakfast
Noon	lunch-dessert
Night	dinner

9–12 MONTHS	
Morning	breakfast
Noon	lunch-dessert
Night	dinner-dessert

FIRST YEAR FEEDING NO-NO'S:

- Sugar, corn syrup, or honey: babies don't need any added sugar, and honey and corn syrup contain botulism spores that can kill infants
- Salt: too hard on little one's kidneys
- Eggs or products with eggs
- Unpasteurized juices: can cause illness or death
- Citrus fruits: too acidic
- Shellfish: can cause allergies and is an acquired, mature taste
- Wheat or corn products: often causes allergies
- Cow's milk: too much protein
- Seeds and nuts, including peanut butter: can cause allergies, and are extreme choking hazards
- Tomatoes and strawberries: often causes allergies

PARENTCRAFT

Diaper Changing

As your baby gets more active, be sure to give him something to play with while you're changing him. There will be less squirming and the process will go faster.

Dressing

So many parents struggle to get their kids dressed starting at this age because they're wriggling around and it becomes this whole trauma just putting on a pair of sweatpants. I think the best thing to do is just to work with the baby, give him something to distract himself with, and do it as quickly as possible.

I also believe in using baby tights from the age of three months upward. Yes, boys and all. Shakespeare did it. Remember, it's all about layering a baby to keep him warm.

Skin Care

As you start introducing solids, if you see an outbreak of "acne," it's probably not. It's probably an allergic reaction from your baby eating something. So be aware very, very quickly and figure out what she's reacting to.

Bathing

I think it's fine for parents to get into the bathtub with their little ones from the 3–6-month mark. There's something quite beautiful about spending time together in the water. You feel confident, and your baby's confident in the water with you. It's a wonderful transition from the small plastic tub to putting them into the big bath by themselves when they can sit up.

Another Form of Babyproofing

You've created a safe environment for your baby through babyproofing, but what about protecting yourself from your baby? I'm talking about hair and earring grabbing and other death-grip activities your little one will now be able to engage in. You can minimize painful situations by wearing your hair back if it is long, and not wearing earrings or necklaces, particularly dangly ones, around your baby. Ditto for ties, Dad. Make sure you take them off before holding him.

I spent years carrying scrunchies on my wrist like bangles so that I could wear my hair down and then pull it up when necessary. (Because sometimes I liked to wear it down to tickle babies with it.) After seventeen years, it's become a habit. Even while filming, I'm always being told to leave my headbands off my wrists.

And if you're one of those moms or dads with lots of piercings, watch out for those as well. Make sure they're studs and not dangling all over the place. Otherwise you just may get caught.

Mouth Care

Once you start feeding solids, you should start mouth cleaning, even if there are no teeth. Those gums are likely getting covered in gunk! You can use a soft infant toothbrush, a piece of wet gauze, or a fingertip brush. No toothpaste though. They all contain fluoride, and swallowing fluoride can harm the enamel of forming teeth.

And remember—no putting your baby to sleep with a bottle in his mouth. That leads to tooth decay, tooth pain, and early loss of milk teeth. Too much milk can alter the process of receiving molars later. Too much milk for the milk teeth.

Out and About

Despite the logistical challenges, taking an infant on a trip is actually easier to do before they're crawling or walking. So consider taking that trip, via plane or car, now. And be sure that your destination is babyproofed.

No matter their age, traveling with children is really all about preparation. It's making sure that you know exactly how long you're gone for, and what the weather is like where you're going so that you have the right clothing, sunblock, shades for the stroller, umbrellas, mosquito net if necessary etc. so they're protected. Make sure you bring extra outfits, not only for your baby, but for you in case of messes. And be sure you get everything in place three days before so you avoid last-minute rushing around.

In seventeen years of nannying, I have very successfully taken many families on vacation and it's been an absolute delight, even when traveling as far as nine or ten hours on a plane with an infant. In addition to good preparation, the key is sticking as much as possible to the baby's routine.

PLANE TRAVEL

Once your baby gets past the first few months and her immune system is a bit more developed, you can consider plane trips. It's a fifty-fifty chance of whether any two flights are the same. Anyone who's sat next to a screaming baby on a long flight knows what I'm talking about. So to increase the chances of a good experience:

- Go at the time your baby is most likely to sleep.
- Call the airline to find out about whether they provide bassinets. Know, however, that if the flight is bumpy, they will ask you to hold your baby in your arms. The safest thing to do it to purchase a seat and strap her in using her car seat.
- Also find out from the airline exactly what you can carry on. Due to security restrictions, this changes often.
- Check your stroller and car seat at the plane door, unless you've bought an airplane seat for your child, in which case bring the car seat on with you.
- Bring lots of powdered formula if you're bottle-feeding, and ask the flight attendants for water to mix it with. The liquid kind or premade bottles may be confiscated at the gate due to liquid restrictions.
- If she's on solids, don't forget to pack those as well.
- Pre-board if possible so you have time and space to settle.
- Feed your baby during takeoff and landing to avoid ear pain due to changes in air pressure.
- Drink extra fluids, especially if you're nursing, to avoid dehydration.
- Put down the diaper pad from your changing bag and change your baby on your seat rather than the cramped, potentially overused bathroom.
- Don't forget to take rattles, favorite toys and baby card books, cloth diaper, and blankie. A few things to do will go a long way toward preserving the sanity of everyone on the plane.

Plane travel with babies doesn't have to be a big, dramatic experience. You can make it easier with preparation and positivity. You're either going to embrace that and have a good experience, or not. The choice is yours. So make it a happy one. At the end of the day, if your baby is crying a lot, remember he's not doing it to annoy everybody on the plane. It's about time people had more consideration with regard to this situation. Babies cry. Let's hope the rest of society can embrace that and be a little bit more compassionate.

CAR TRIPS

Many families find car trips easier with infants because you have the flexibility of being able to stop anywhere and take a breather. And the motion of the car normally gets babies sleeping really well.

Car trips are also good because you also don't have the added pressure of everybody looking over at you if your baby is crying, as it's just you and your family in the car. I think to some degree that does allow parents to feel a little bit more relaxed, as they don't have to worry about those around them.

The list of what to bring is the same as for the plane.

STIMULATION AND EXPLORATIONS

You're a bit of a stimulation pro now, aren't you? You know what makes your baby laugh, what makes him giggle and grin, as well as what activities he doesn't enjoy. He's developing fast. Not only can he see much better, he's able to reach out for things, pull objects close, shake them, drop them with intent, put them in his mouth. It's a whole different ball game now.

So it's important to continue the activities you've been doing while adding more play to develop her motor skills. You'll be getting more feedback from now on, and the interaction you have with your baby will be really rewarding for you as she becomes more adventurous.

Have a Conversation

Now's the time to begin to encourage a baby's communication skills by having a conversation. Imitate what your baby is saying. If she makes a high-pitched sound, do the same. Soon she'll start to repeat the sounds you make. This helps promote language, listening, and social development. Plus you'll have fun too. You don't know what you're saying, but you do know what you're saying, and that's what's so beautiful about it.

More Tummy Time

Your baby's neck muscles are a lot stronger now and are able to support his head. It's important to build that upper body strength. So a great thing to do with him is to have him balance on his tummy on a bolster or an inflatable beach ball (with you holding on of course). Talk to him so he gets engrossed in what you're saying so he will go longer and longer with that tummy time.

Another thing to do while he's on his tummy is place a plastic ball in front of him and encourage him to stretch out for it. Make it really attractive to him by shaking it a few inches away. If he's got his fingers on it, don't take it away from him. Otherwise it's going to be very disheartening because it takes a lot of energy for a baby to reach out and grab that ball. So be aware of the amount of time you spend doing this, because it can be very tiring. Imagine us spending three hours in the gym. Need I say more?

A lot of parents feel uncomfortable hearing their child make those grunts of determination as she reaches for something and go in and rescue. It's important to let her try because it develops the will to keep trying. Nothing was ever achieved with being able to quit easily. So allow your baby to strive with determination to get what she wants. Unless she gets very frustrated and wails, of course. The reward comes when you see your baby smile with satisfaction from actually having been able to reach out and grab that ball: it's mine, I've got it.

Grasp and Release

At 3–6 months, your baby is going to be able to hold things, but not for long. You can help develop his eye-hand coordination and fine motor skills by giving him plastic spoons or keys, Tupperware, rattles, etc. to grab onto. Soon he'll drop it, but the more he practices grasp and release, the better he'll get at it.

Superman

Rumor has it that it's not safe to throw your baby up into the air and catch her. So I'm not asking you to throw your baby up in the air like a football. But you can lie on your back on the floor with your baby and hold her at arm's length over your head and fly her around. It's great for developing trust as she enjoys that feeling of being up in the air and you supporting her safely.

Bubbles

Who doesn't love bubbles? Bubbles are great because you're able to have so much fun with them in vast amounts and they really do allow your baby to develop eye-hand coordination. Obviously you don't want to blow so many at your baby that she ends up swallowing them.

Bubbles are also a fabulous distraction if your baby's upset.

Dancing Ribbons

With babies this age, I love to take lots of colorful different ribbons and wave them in front of him. By six months, he's able to hold onto the ribbons as they flutter. This develops eye-hand coordination and allows you to build up those happy memories between the two of you.

Hiding Games

Now's also the time for hiding games: take a block and hide it under his blanket for a second with a corner hanging out, and then bring it back out. You'll be amazed at how astounded he is. These hiding and throwing things down games should go on for many months as your infant learns more and more about object permanence, the fact that things (and people) are there even when you can't see them.

Reading

It's never too soon to start reading to her. She loves the sound of your voice, and those infant books with the large, colorful pictures are great for her visual stimulation. The more you link pictures with words, the easier it will be for her to do so when she's a toddler. Try the board or cloth ones that are age-appropriate.

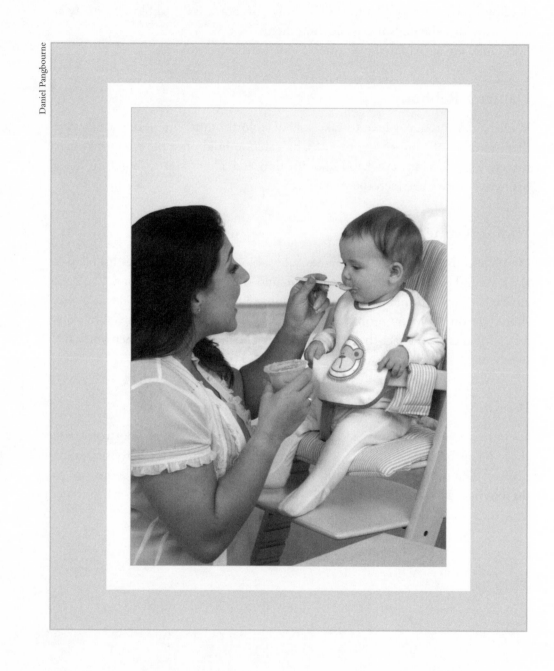

CHAPTER 6

Six to Nine Months

 PARENTS' JOURNEY

You may find that, in a way, life up to this point was relatively easy because you just breast-fed and slept next to him and could carry him wherever you wanted to go. Then one day this baby, who has just sat there propped up with pillows like a little Buddha, decides to shock you and disappears. It's a whole different ball game now. He's mobile! For some it's between 6–9 months; for others, later. Whenever it happens, it means you'll be on your feet more, keeping him safe as he makes his rounds. It's going to be harder to contain him in order to do what you need to do.

Once again, you're in a learning curve and will have to adapt. Your routines will have to be flexible to be able to take his new mobility into consideration as well. The good news is that you've got a half year of experience now, so lots of the routine things, like bathing and changing, should be second nature. In a lot of ways, you're already a pro. Now you're going to apply your experience to a much more excited, rolling, and moving baby. Because for him it's like, wow! Look where my legs can take me.

This is when you grow eyes in the back of your head. You wake up one morning, feel two lumps and you recognize it's not a headache. There are two eyeballs back there. (If only!)

You're into a different layer of the parental cake of concern. Up till now you've been concerned with whether he's getting enough food and sleeping through the night. Now it's about keeping him safe from getting injured or putting something dangerous in his mouth: "Oh my God! What's he going to break this time? Is that the dog food he's eating?" Even though you've babyproofed it will become more apparent how important it is, as many parents don't get it until now.

This is also a different stage for parents because there's much more interaction and feedback from the baby. A wonderful rapport builds because she's mimicking your facial expression and tones. You're able to have semi-conversations. By nine months, she's really come into her own with her personality. You don't just make her laugh anymore; she makes you laugh, as well.

While you've entered into a new phase with mobility, at the same time you're definitely more confident in the way that you're handling your baby. You've probably weathered some phone calls or visits to the doctor about sniffles or other illnesses. You're making conscious choices about what he wears and who he plays with and may have introduced Mommy & Me classes.

Most likely at some time during this period, he'll begin to cut his teeth. Oh my dear, the diaper is unlike any other diaper when a child is teething. You just never thought it possible that your child would *ever, ever* leave you with this horrible mess. The smell is unlike any other. Where's the gas mask?

Suddenly, your sweet baby may be irritable, and you go through another phase of not being able to console him so easily. As a result, you can again feel so helpless. When your child is in pain and there's very little you can do, it really hurts. You can't take the pain for him, but you feel it! Your empathy really starts to grow here as you experience, not for the last time, what it's like to feel your child's pain. The best thing you can do is offer your comfort and know that this time will pass.

Socializing Time

Beginning now, you'll be more active in the world again. It's back to normal, give or take your baby's routine. This is the time for you and your baby to get out in the world for:

- regular coffee mornings
- Mommy & Me classes

- playdates with other babies in parks, places of worship, and homes
- lunch dates with other babies so they can eat finger foods

Going Back to Work

While some mothers go back to work when their babies are younger or older, it's often during this time frame that women have to leave their babies, either full- or part-time. This can be a very difficult emotional transition. Hopefully, you've taken my advice in Chapter 2 and found someone whom you really trust.

How you deal with your own emotions is going to be a process that takes time. There are some things you can do that help. First, don't feel bad if you call 100 times in the beginning to check on your little one. Tell your caregiver that you will eventually wean off the frequency. Have her keep a log or diary so that you can see what your baby's doing on a daily basis, which will help you to feel you're not missing out on his growth, as you know what's going on. Make sure you have someone to talk to about how you're feeling. It's natural to feel sadness and/or guilt for a period of time.

Recognize what you can and cannot change! You cannot change that you need to work. But by recognizing that your baby is your priority, you can make work decisions around that. Can you drive him there and back? Can you make sure you're there before he goes to sleep in the evening? Can you avoid business travel the first year? Can you work one day a week from home?

If, after a month or two, you still don't feel okay and the situation is affecting you to the point where you're extremely anxious or depressed, then I would definitely question the bigger picture. Is it the place you're leaving your baby? Or is this a situation where you and your partner need to start looking at other options so that Mom can work part-time?

I once looked after a baby for six months, and the mother came home every day and was fine. Then over a period of six weeks or so, every evening she came home I thought, "She's just not quite right." She seemed vague and an inner sadness was present. Finally I pulled her aside and said, "You don't have to necessarily share it with me, but I get the sense you're unhappy." She burst into tears, saying, "I want to stay home with my baby. But I feel so bad because I hired you for a year. I haven't discussed it with my husband, but I know we would be fine financially if I did. Work is not the same now that I have my little one."

I replied, "It's your baby. You must do what makes you happy so that you can be the best parent you can, and your baby will be happier too. I'm gone tomorrow!" It was one time I felt so glad to leave, as it's always hard to say good-bye to a family you've built a relationship with.

If you've got a career and a baby, you've got some juggling to do. You can't be a successful businessperson and not put the time in. Something always has to give a little. So tell yourself the truth and work through it.

The first year is all about bonding. So make sure that the time that you do have with your child is spent in connecting emotionally, so that you don't feel withdrawal symptoms. Because that's what parents feel when they work—withdrawal symptoms of not being able to bond on a moment-by-moment basis with their child. So make that your priority when you are at home.

The same for having fun, fun, fun. You've got to be enjoying parenthood and spending good quality time with your little nipper.

DEVELOPMENTAL OVERVIEW

Physical

During this time, his head growth is slowing. By eight months, your baby should weigh somewhere between 13½–18 pounds.

In the seventh month, he can sit on his own for some time, although he usually can't get himself into a sitting position until eight months. Soon when he topples over, he'll use his arms to catch himself.

He loves to stand while you hold him and bounce up and down, and he can move objects from hand to hand. By the ninth month, he will start using his thumb to hold things, and will put his finger into holes.

When he first starts to stand, at about eight months, he won't know how to get back down and you may find him crying for help. Gently bend his knees to get him back down.

When standing, both her tummy and bum stick out so that her back has quite a sway to it. That's perfectly normal until the second year and has to do with developing balance. Her toes may also point in or out, which also should straighten out in the second year. Teach her to fall on her bottom by pushing gently on her tummy to make her knees buckle. She'll go boom. If you smile and laugh, she will too. Help her up and do it again. The idea is to help her learn that she can fall and be okay. Of course, make sure she can't hit her head on anything before you do it. And remember, a gentle push.

Typically around seven months, babies begin to crawl, although some skip this phase altogether and move straight from sitting to walking with

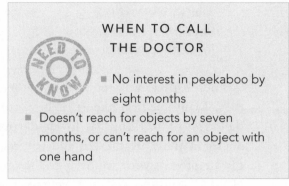

WHEN TO CALL THE DOCTOR

- No interest in peekaboo by eight months
- Doesn't reach for objects by seven months, or can't reach for an object with one hand

no ill effects. Others scoot around on their bums doing what I call the bottom shuffle. Others slither like snakes on their tummies. Many crawl backward first like little remote cars because their arms are stronger than their legs.

In terms of brain development, he's learning to solve his own problems through experimentation. So you'll begin to see him try something a few times different ways before giving up. He's learning to set a goal, ignore distractions, and persist. And he'll remember what worked before!

Teething

Typically this is the period where babies begin to cut their teeth. Whenever your baby's first tooth comes in, beware, breast-feeding moms—you will probably get bitten. If you cry out, it will probably startle him too. If he keeps doing it, calmly unlatch him and let a few seconds pass before allowing him to latch on again. After a few times of this, most babies get the message.

Times can be hard, for you and for them, when babies are teething. Teething signs include:

- drooling/dribbling
- hot, itchy, red, swollen gums or a bluish blister (eruption cyst)
- irritability
- chewing on anything
- loss of appetite
- sporadic trouble sleeping
- red cheeks with fine lines that look like a tic-tac-toe game

- aching, sporadic cry
- slight fever
- loose poopy diapers

There's disagreement as to whether teething causes either fever or diarrhea. Many medical experts believe something else is going on, perhaps that the stress of teething has lowered your baby's immunity. Check with your doctor if these are present and you're concerned. It's my opinion that both can be present with teething and it's nothing that can't be handled with lots of TLC, teething aids, and Pedialyte, an electrolyte replacement liquid that prevents dehydration.

Teeth can take up to two months to break through the gums and babies can be in acute pain and letting you know it with screams and cries. Oral gels work, but beware of overuse. Painkillers such as baby Advil and Tylenol can also be used. Never give a child aspirin under any circumstances. It is associated with a potentially life-threatening condition called Reye's syndrome that attacks all the organs of the body, particularly the brain and liver, and can develop from a flu, cold, or other disease when a baby is given aspirin.

You can also try teething rings, a cold washcloth, gel packs, or just rub your finger on his gums. Keep his bottom and chin clean and dry, and give lots of cuddles.

Be aware that if your baby bites you, he's not doing it on purpose but because it helps relieve the pressure of teething. You can tell him "no biting" so he knows not to do it again.

Social/Emotional

At seven months, she is able to remember someone's face. By eight months, she's beginning to make the connection between tones and words and gestures—like bye-bye and waving. She probably loves toys that make noise by banging or shaking.

By nine months, he can follow simple commands like, "wave bye-bye," point to what he wants, and is familiar with the word and tone *no*. He may want to "help" with eating now—dipping fingers in and smearing food, holding a spoon or bottle. This may make it harder to feed him, but it's an important step to eating independently. By nine months, he's able to finger feed and drink from a sippy cup with your help. He also can now express preferences by pushing away things he doesn't want, or grabbing hold of the things he does.

Eight to nine months is when stranger anxiety tends to really kick in. He will probably have a preference for those he already knows, especially the primary carer, and may cry fiercely when a stranger gets close. Give him time to get used to new people by having them approach slowly over time and by your showing pleasure at their arrival. You may also find he smiles only for you and other family members he's spent a long time with. By ten months, this stage is usually at its peak.

He may also be suddenly afraid of heights or of the bath. You may also notice your baby becomes more irritable right before a big jump in development, like crawling. This is perfectly normal. So is resisting sleep—bedtime and naps. Life is just so exciting and challenging!

BABYPROOFING

Now that she's in motion, make sure you've safety-proofed the house adequately per my recommendations in the 3–6 month babyproofing section. In the blink of an eye, she can tumble down the stairs, put a finger in an electric socket, choke on a small battery, or drown in an inch of water.

Bottom line when your baby's in motion: It's a fine balance between creating a safe environment and going overboard. You need to decide what you're going to get out of the way and what you're going to teach your child about. For instance, some people say, "We've got a cat. And the cat is always going to be there and the cat food's always going to be there. So we're going to teach our baby, 'Come away from there, that's the cat food' instead of putting it out of reach."

That's why this stage is about recognizing what things you want to remain so you're going to teach your child to avoid them and what are the things that you're going to put up or away until they're older. If you can make the distinction, you're halfway there. But don't expect to have a palace. After all, you have kids, and you don't want to keep telling them no.

Standing Hazards

Now that she can stand, make sure the crib and changing table are not by a window as it is very dangerous. First you have this immobile baby and then all of a sudden, it's like "Da-dum! Mission impossible!" Off she goes! Changing her on a pad on the floor eliminates the danger.

This is the time to take away mobiles too—so that he can't stand up, pull it down, and get tangled. This is the time to lower the mattress to the lowest setting so he can't fall out easily, and remove any large toys he can stand on to boost himself up and out. Get rid of bumpers now too, because he can stand on those to get out as well.

Crawling Hazards

Get down on the floor for a crawling baby's-eye view of the world to make sure you've eliminated all dangers: tippy vases or lamps on coffee tables, your favorite knickknacks, tablecloths, top-heavy chairs, and the like. Be sure the TV can't fall or be pulled off whatever it's on. This is about not only keeping your baby safe, but your things, as well. As your baby becomes mobile, he will want to explore his world as much as possible. And you don't want to have to worry about Aunt Tilly's fancy vase getting smashed. Not to mention your dear little one getting hurt. She's not going to think, "Ohhhh! That's a Wedgwood! I better leave that one alone! Let me go and just touch the one from IKEA!" She is not aware of how hard you worked to place that on the side table. She'll have it down like she's knocking coconuts at the fair. I've also seen people who have their lovely display of wines in racks ready to pull out. And pull them out, she will. Put anything you consider precious away, and put the household stuff in appropriately high places!

Put his books and toys on low shelves and move the things you want to preserve to the top ones. Make sure tall furniture is bolted to the wall so your baby can't pull it over on himself. Be sure to keep dresser doors closed, or you may find them being used as climbing devices. You can get the wedges that go over the doors so the door never really closes and he can't jam his fingers in them. They look like big foamy *C*'s.

You can buy edge and corner cushions to avoid bumps and bruises, and use foam tape around the edges of glass tables. Block off furniture that he can crawl under and get stuck in. When babies start to crawl, they're not like cats. They don't have whiskers to determine the width of something, so they go in somewhere and can't get back out again. Sometimes babies will crawl forward and then realize: "How do I reverse to get back out?" You have to pull them out, which always makes me laugh.

Keep appliances unplugged as much as possible and don't allow cords to dangle. Have discussions with your partner about getting alarms on the dangerous doors and windows.

> **NEED TO KNOW**
>
> ## NANNY NO-NO'S ANIMAL AVOIDANCE
>
> There are a number of animals that babies should not come in contact with because they have been found to carry salmonella and other dangerous illnesses:
>
> - baby chicks and ducklings
> - toads and frogs
> - turtles
> - lizards
> - snakes

Place guards in front of fireplaces and steam radiators, and remove space and kerosene heaters. Tie up cords to blinds and drapes so he can't reach them, or use a cleat in the wall to make sure nothing's dangling. Hanging cords are a strangulation hazard.

Be even more careful about pets now that he can move. His crawling can scare your cat or dog and cause aggression. So make sure you're always around your child and pet.

In the Bathroom

Consider installing a safety latch on your toilet lid so that she can't fall in if you've got a baby that's fascinated with the toilet. Toilets are dangerous because babies are top-heavy—if they lean over, they can tumble in.

Keep makeup, medicines, toothpaste, razors, tweezers, curling irons, hair dryers, etc. out of reach. Be aware of where you put your little perfumed goodies, because for your little one, it looks like a colored drink in a bottle. Those oils look appealing because they're bright and colorful. Babies will put them in their mouths. Perfumes, because they have alcohol, are particularly poisonous. Train yourself to put them out of reach and close the bathroom door behind you.

In the Kitchen

Make sure the garbage can has a tight lid on it. Keep all vitamins out of reach— iron poisoning is the most common cause of infant poisoning death. Don't let her play with the knobs on the stove and be mindful of the oven door as it gets hot. Ditto for iron and ironing board. And if you have pets, the food and water bowls are tempting targets for a crawling baby. Be sure to put them somewhere he can't get to. The same for cat litter boxes—you definitely don't want him getting into that!

Most burns of children aged six months to two years come from spilling of hot liquids and foods. So keep your little one in a safe spot in the kitchen, as far away from ovens and appliances as possible. I advise putting him in a baby gym next to a little wicker basket full of his toys to occupy him while you're cooking. At eight and nine months, babies need engaging all the time. If he's on the loose, put him in a safe corner with toys and if he crawls to you, make sure you take him back out of harm's way.

In addition to safety reasons, the high chair next to the stove is a problem because you're more likely to give your baby food to keep him quiet, as you're not able to give him attention. This sets up a link between comfort or distraction and eating. Don't pacify with food!

No Out of Sight

These points are here for you to become aware of what you need to always be aware of. Once your eyes are open, you're never going to think, "I can sit back and let my baby crawl all over the house by himself." Know exactly what's in every room that may be a danger. At this stage, your child shouldn't be anywhere by himself so long that he could, for instance, go to the washing machine, undo the door, and get in. As soon as he turns a corner—eek-eek-eek—you can't see him, then you need to go after him. If he's crawled off the radar screen, Mom and Dad, go get him.

SETTING FIRM GROUND

Solid Sleep

By now you have a few things in place for a solid sleep routine: She's in her crib, in her own room, or separated by some kind of light and noise divider from others, and on solid foods.

It's important that you place him in his crib awake; otherwise you start to create bad habits. Your child gets used to falling asleep in your arms and then when he wakes up, he becomes very fretful because you're no longer there.

By now, your baby will be awake more of the time. That's wonderful. But you need to make sure she has two sleeps during the day, one in the morning and one in the afternoon, which last between an hour and two hours each.

Be aware that at around eight months, her sleep might start to be disrupted. You'll find her testing boundaries regarding sleeping around eight months and again at thirteen months.

SLEEP ROUTINE: 6–9 MONTHS	
You're looking to gradually adjust the schedule over the three months, beginning with the first and ending with the second.	
Age	Activity
6 months	
	play
	mid-morning nap (2 hours)
	play
	afternoon nap (2 hours)
	play
	bedtime (10–12 hours)

(continued on next page)

SLEEP ROUTINE: 6–9 MONTHS

9 months

      play

      mid-morning nap (1 hour)

      play

      afternoon nap (2½ hours)

      play

      bedtime (10–12 hours)

Controlled Crying Technique

Now that she's on solid foods, she will be able to go to sleep on her own and stay asleep through the night. The importance of getting your baby to sleep through the night is crucial so you're not being sleep deprived. To avoid going in to comfort your child dozens of times, use my controlled crying technique. I've used it to great success with six-month-old babies up to toddlers. Use it first for naps, then nighttime.

You need a timer and a strong resolve. The first time he cries, go in, reassure him, and then leave. Wait five minutes and if he's still crying, go back in and repeat the routine. Then wait ten minutes and return if necessary, then twenty. In other words, you double the time each time. Soon you'll have a baby who can soothe himself to sleep without you.

When you go in to say *shhhhh*, just rest your hand on her without eye contact and then leave. Do not pick her up or it will lead her to think she's getting out of bed. Some babies will cry and start to gag. If he throws up, take him from his crib, clean him up, and place back in the crib. Then do the technique again.

If you've got a baby who's in a crib in your room because you don't want to put him with your six-year-old, you would still do the same technique, but with you in the room. If he wakes in the night crying and you are lying in bed, you would wait the five minutes and then you would go over, lay him down, and say, "*Shhhh.*" And then you go to ten, etc. just as I described before. It is going to be harder because he can see you. And he's screaming like nobody's business right near you. If you keep at it though, he will learn.

Whether in your room or not, the consistency of the technique helps it work, along with making sure that she's getting lots of love, attention, and stimulation during waking hours. This healthy balance will allow your child to recognize that there are times when she needs to go to sleep. If your child is getting all she needs from you during the day, this technique of active ignoring is not neglect. Rather, it is teaching her in a healthy way to soothe herself to sleep, and that's an important process for every child to learn.

FEEDING

You want to be serving solid foods at more than one meal now because your baby needs more nutrients. Refer to my chart on pages 130–31 in Feeding 3–6 months for the order of introducing solids at meals.

By the end of nine months or so, you may find that his need to breast- or bottle-feed will begin to taper off until it's once in the morning and once in the evening, depending on the decisions you make. This is a natural progression that will help your baby get all the nutrition he needs. If you keep offering only breast milk or formula all day, he may not get hungry enough to eat the solids he needs.

Babies at this age still need to eat every 3–4 hours, so if you are introducing regular mealtimes, be sure to offer snacks mid-morning and mid-afternoon as well. Don't force-feed those snacks. I suggest you follow the feeding routine here:

FEEDING SCHEDULE: 6–9 MONTHS

Now you're introducing food as well as more formula
or breast milk at a time.
Bottle feeders should start at four bottles and go to two
over the three months.

Time	Activity
6:30 AM	breast-feed 20–40 minutes or bottle-feed 8 oz.
8:30 AM	breakfast
10:30 AM	breast-feed 20–40 minutes or bottle-feed 6 oz.

(continued on next page)

FEEDING SCHEDULE: 6–9 MONTHS

Time	Activity
1:00 P M	lunch
2:00 P M	breast-feed 20–40 minutes or bottle-feed 6 oz.
4:30 P M	dinner
6:00 P M	breast-feed 20–40 minutes or bottle-feed 8 oz.
6:00 A M	breast-feed 20–40 minutes or bottle-feed 8–9 oz.
8:30 A M	breakfast
10:00 A M	breast-feed 20–40 minutes or bottle-feed 6 oz.
12:00 P M	lunch
1:30 P M	breast-feed 20–40 minutes or bottle-feed 6 oz.
3:30 P M	snack
4:30 P M	breast-feed 20–40 minutes or bottle-feed 6–8 oz.
6:30 P M	breast-feed 20–40 minutes or bottle-feed 8–9 oz.
7:00 A M	breast-feed 20–40 minutes or bottle-feed 9 oz.
9:30 A M	breakfast
1:00 P M	lunch/dessert
3:30 P M	snack/yogurt
5:00 P M	dinner
6:30 P M	breast-feed 20–40 minutes or bottle-feed 8 oz.

SLEEPY TIME FOODS

Did you know that certain foods, like oatmeal and turkey, tend to create sleepiness? It's due to the presence of tryptophan, a chemical that produces drowsiness. That's why at Thanksgiving we fall asleep at the table.

As your baby's teeth come in and he is able to sit up well in a high chair, you can begin to serve finger foods, which are great for his fine motor skills and pincer grip. Keep in mind the food no-no's on page 131 and the choking hazards following. Parents may be surprised to learn that babies can use their gums to mash quite a few foods. Stews

GOOD FINGER FOODS, 6–9 MONTHS

All food should be cored, seeded, and cut into small pieces

- Fruits: Apples, apricots, avocado, banana (a piece of frozen banana is great for teething babies), mango, melon, nectarine, papaya, peach, pear

- Dried fruit is a good source of iron, but don't give too much. Soak it in boiling water to soften it if baby finds it difficult to chew

- Vegetables: Steamed eggplant, green beans, broccoli, cabbage, carrots, cauliflower, celery, peas, potato, sweet corn, sweet peppers, sweet potato

- Other foods: Bread dipped in fruit or vegetable purees are good when baby refuses to be spoon-fed

- Miniature sandwiches filled with mashed banana, chopped chicken with fruit chutney, cottage cheese and grated apple, cream cheese and strawberry jam

- Start with grated cheese. Once chewing is mastered, move on to very small pieces, then strips. Avoid strong cheeses such as blue, Brie, and Camembert. Make sure the cheese is pasteurized

- Pasta in all shapes and sizes with a vegetable puree, and maybe grated cheese on top

- Strips of chicken are good, especially if they have been cooked in a sauce so they're tender

- White filleted fish, bones carefully removed, cooked in sauce is also good

- Braised beef and vegetables, and other meats made soft and tender in a crockpot by slow cooking

are clearly too messy. Cereals, bread, and crackers are fine for snacks, but they have too much sugar and starches to be given as a meal. You want your baby to be getting vitamins and protein. Try minute pieces of banana, chicken, beef, lamb, or pork, cooked carrots, peas, or green beans, cheese (but never the mold-ripened soft kinds like Brie or blue). Keep to foods that are au naturel—no artificial flavors or coloring. Again, introduce foods one at a time and make sure you offer variety. Don't keep pushing just the applesauce. A new food every week or so is a good pace. If he doesn't like something, try serving it for a couple days. If he still rejects it, try it again in a week or so.

She will eat a nice portion of food now at each feeding. Generally children know when they are full, especially when they're young. Trust her to show you when she's had enough. Also be aware that babies eat in spurts—don't expect her to consume the same quantity each meal.

PREVENTING CHOKING

To make sure she doesn't choke on her food, be sure your baby is sitting up to eat, and is not laughing or talking. Never feed in the car. If you stop suddenly she can choke.

Don't allow her to stuff her mouth. Cut all food, including small round food like peas and grapes, into pieces no larger than half the size of the bed of your little fingernail, and avoid altogether the following choking hazards:

- whole grapes
- whole hot dogs or sausages
- popcorn, potato chips, and pretzels
- marshmallows
- raisins
- nuts and seeds
- hard candies, including lollipops

- peanut butter
- raw vegetables, including carrot and celery sticks
- chewing gum
- raw firm fruits, like apples and pears
- ice cubes
- flaky fish chunks
- ice cream cones, which can stick to the back of the mouth

As your baby reaches the nine-month mark, it's the time to begin to serve liquids in a sippy cup. Plastic no-spill sippy cups are great to begin with because they have no handles and a soft spout. I suggest you offer water. If you offer juice, even diluted, babies quickly prefer it because it's sweet. No need to encourage a sweet tooth! Keep mostly to water.

Make sure your baby is wearing a bib, which will save you from washing clothes each mealtime. I love the big plastic ones that have a scoop because I get a great kick out of watching babies concentrate on picking food out of it and feeling pleased with themselves for achieving that.

At around nine months, she'll watch you and copy you. As you open your mouth to eat, she'll open hers: "Here comes the choo-choo, in it goes, bye-bye." Make sure you don't have toys on her high chair tray while feeding; it makes the whole process much harder if she's trying to play. Give him a plastic spoon to hold, even if all he does is bang it on the table while the other spoon goes in. Eventually he'll figure out what to do with it. Yogurt containers are good for little ones to play around with as they are easy to hold and wide enough to get a spoon in.

PARENTCRAFT

Dressing

Remember my rule of thumb for working *with* your baby when dressing. The older she gets, the more she's not going to want to lie down. So once she can sit up on her own, don't lie her down to get her dressed all the time. Instead, let her sit up and put the top over her head. Change the scenery as well. Don't always dress her in the same place and the same position. You'll find you'll get less resistance.

Bathing

Once your baby can sit up confidently, he can graduate to one of those ring seats in the big bathtub—with you holding on and never leaving for a second, of course. Or once he's a solid sitter, you can just place him in the big tub.

From about six months onward, bathing is not just about hygiene, but having fun and creating confidence with water. Of course there are lots of squeaky toys, ones that you burp up, ones that squeak, ones that splash water. Bath times can really become something babies relish, not just as part of their routine but for fun as well.

A few tips for making it a fun and safe experience:

- Make sure the room is nice and warm. If it's slightly humid, that helps babies, especially in the winter if they've got slight breathing problems and to counteract the dryness of the season.
- Get everything ready you need for when she gets out of the bath.
- Put down a nonslip bath mat inside and outside the bath.
- The less confident you feel, the less water you should have. You never want a swimming pool, but you can graduate to a bit more water as you get used to the awkwardness of bending over and holding on as you wash.
- Test the water to make sure it's not too hot or cold.
- Always hold on; you don't want him to slip.
- Consider getting a guard for the faucet so he won't hurt his head on it.
- Use liquid soap and shampoo, because babies have been known to choke on bits of bar soap.
- Get her used to having a sponge on her head very gently with water trickling down.
- Keep a big towel by your side to wrap her in when she comes out.

Diapering

Sometimes, beginning at around eight months, babies will stick their hands in the poo when you're changing them if you're not fast enough to catch them. Quick things! By this time in their lives, they are usually pooing three times a day, morning, afternoon, and night. If you pay attention, you will minimize the mess. No matter what, stay calm. Just wash her hands and say in a calm voice, "That's poo-poo. Not on your hands, stay in diaper."

At about this time, he may resist getting his diaper changed. It's taking up too much of his day and he'd rather be playing. Again, the main thing is to give him a good distraction, something to hold on to while he's having his diaper changed or talking to him.

Dining Out

As he gets into solid food and becomes more active, eating out with him will be messier and more challenging. The key is to create a fun experience for you and your child. Go for a family-friendly restaurant, and keep it short and sweet. If you create a fun experience, it allows you to feel competent enough to do it again.

Bring a few things for her to play with: blocks, books, finger puppets. And of course there's always, "I drop it and you pick it up."

Play it by ear. You might want to feed her before, then let her have a few finger foods at the table. Remember about time: an eight-month-old cannot sit as long as an adult. Don't expect to have a three-course meal. By now she's on a very consistent routine as well, so you know you only have a certain amount of time before she starts to get tired. However, there's no reason why she can't get out of the high chair and into the stroller and lay back if she really starts to get sleepy.

Beware of the crayons they often give out at family restaurants because of course he's going to want to pop them in his mouth. A definite no-no.

Harnessing

He's more mobile now, so be sure to strap him into any stroller, grocery cart, high chair, etc. You may be encountering the "no no" shaking of head, body stiff as a board, temper tantrums, whether that's in car rides, plane flights, or grocery trips.

Those screams can be incredibly stressful on you. Start by figuring out if he's wet or hungry, or whether something's pinching him. Is he too hot? Cold? If you've taken care of all those needs and it's being confined that's the problem, try distractions: a toy, a song, jiggle the seat. Try peekaboo while strapping him in. Make sure he has enough playtime before getting into the car.

Whatever you do, remain calm. He's too young to reason with. Sometimes these moments simply have to be endured. Just do what you need to do.

Above all, don't give in to "What kind of parent will everyone think I am if my child is screaming?" It doesn't matter that everyone's looking. Here's one of your first chances to ask yourself: What kind of a parent am I? One who's going to not do the right thing because other people are going to look at me, or one they're going to look at and think, "Why aren't you doing anything?" It's your job to do the right thing for your child, whether he likes it or not, and whether it creates a scene or not. There are some crucial things he's not going to like, but are final. Harnesses in carts are one!

STIMULATION AND EXPLORATIONS

Ready, world, here comes baby! This time is about continuing to support fine and gross motor development so that crawling and walking come along nicely, as well as keeping the auditory and visual stimulation going.

Keep Talking!

Take the sounds he's making—da, da, for instance—and turn it into words for him: daddy, bottle, etc. He may not say his first recognizable word until a year or so, but he understands your tone much earlier.

Narrate what you're doing as you care for him. Be sure your language is simple and concrete. Describe what's happening: "Now we're taking a bath. Does the water feel good? Here comes the soap . . ." Label everything as you use it: "Want the spoon now?" Pause as if you were having a conversation with an adult and wait for a response. You may get only a "ga-ga," but he's learning the give-and-take of conversation, and your expectation that he will speak encourages him to do so.

Footie

Okay, I'm not promising you that your baby is going to turn into the next David Beckham, but I don't know any baby of this age who doesn't love a game of footie. Hold your baby securely in front of you and position her legs on the top of a ball and make it roll across the floor. This works on eye-foot coordination and gross motor skills. Of course, it's not going to be until she's two, two and a half years old, that she's actually going to be able to kick the ball by herself. You're providing the muscle power. She's getting to kick her legs, gurgle, and enjoy the experience.

Head and Shoulders

When babies are born, they have no sense that they are separate beings from their mothers. There's no conscious awareness, but the more they move around, the more they start to realize they are their own person.

To reinforce this you can play peekaboo in the mirror and identify body parts: "Here is Mommy's eye, here is Max's eye." Or just touch a body part and name it, or sing the old "Head, Shoulders, Knees, and Toes." Babies love it.

A Soft Landing

When you're playing with your child and she starts sitting up by holding her hands in front of her looking like a tripod, then lifts her hands up and starts to fall over, it's important to let that happen while cushioning the fall with your hands so she doesn't get hurt. This allows her not to feel scared. Her balance will soon get better and it won't happen any more.

Obstacle Course

Isn't it funny the way your baby is beginning to crawl? Some babies bottom-shuttle backward. They remind me of little windup plastic babies. They go over things rather than around. They have no special concepts, so they just go forward or just go backward. What fun!

You can encourage crawling by placing things right in front so that your baby will crawl over to that particular thing he's interested in. Get down on the floor with him and let him crawl over you. As he gets more adept, create obstacle courses with small pillows, couch cushions, and boxes. Put him at one end of a tunnel and your face at the other end so he can crawl to you as you encourage him.

Add in peekaboo by hiding behind an object. Make sure you are constantly with him while doing this because he can get stuck under a box, which can be frightening, or covered by a cushion. And be sure to pick it up when done so he doesn't get caught.

Puppet Shows

As babies reach the nine-month mark, I like to put on finger puppets and entertain my little charges. Add music and you can put on a musical show. It allows you to interact with your baby on a social level, and because she's more in tune with her visual tracking, she'll be able to see exactly what's in front of her and to grasp for it.

Food Fun

You can play all sorts of games while feeding. One of my favorites is where the spoon is a train and you pretend you don't know where it's gone as the baby engulfs that spoonful, relishing in the delight that she's swallowed it and you don't know where it is. She'll love your surprised face.

A Drawer of Her Own

As your baby becomes mobile, she's going to become curious about the world around her, so be sure to have a dedicated place with safe objects for her to explore. Leave one of the bottom kitchen drawers full of Tupperware and plastic cups and measuring spoons that is hers to rummage through.

His pincer grasp will develop around eight months, so he'll love to pick up objects now using thumb and forefinger. Give him an object like a set of measuring spoons and a large container from his drawer and show him how to drop them into the container and how to take them out again. He'll want to do it over and over. Remember, repetition is the name of the baby game.

Keep a set of stacking cups in there too. She'll love to bang them together and to hear the noise. She's becoming aware that she can create that noise for herself.

Old-fashioned Games

I love all those games we did with our grandmothers and they did with their parents. Like:

- Ride a horse to Banberry Cross, where you've got your child on your lap and you're bouncing them up and down;
- Humpty Dumpty sat on the wall, where you have them go *fall* . . . (while still holding on, of course);
- Twinkle, twinkle, little star;
- Eensy-weensy spider;
- Row, row, row your boat, where you hold their hands and rock back and forth.

All these games allow you to physically connect with your child in a way that is fun and exciting, as well as good for her development.

Activity Boards, Baby Gym Rings, and Pop-up Toys

I'm a firm believer in activity boards, baby gym rings, and pop-up toys starting at 6–9 months. They help develop her fine motor skills and discover cause and effect: push this and the duck goes quack. The pop-ups also allow her to begin to understand object permanence. In order to help him learn the amounts of pressure he needs to put on the button so that it actually works, just put your hand over his and say, "Press down" or "Flip this," whatever movement it is.

I also love activity boards because they allow your baby to explore on her own. Up until now, everything you've been doing has involved you. But these toys allow your baby to play solo. And that's a crucial ability to develop!

Although she may start fussing as soon as you put her down, it's important for her to get comfortable sitting on her own propped up with cushions for a moment. Try settling her in a baby gym with an activity board while you're preparing lunch or grabbing a quick coffee. You can stay close and talk to her so that she knows that you're there. Gradually increase your distance and the duration of minutes so that by the time she's nine months, you can get up from the sitting room to go and put in a load of wash and then come back again on your own because you know she's going to be okay on her own (in a safety-proofed environment, of course).

Baby gym rings are also great when you have another parent and baby around and you put both babies into the ring. They're able to have fun with the things in the rings, while they're beginning social development. Have you ever watched two young babies together? First they don't notice one another, then they look very intensely. Then you start to see them babble and touch each other. Hello, you! It's absolutely delightful to see.

The Big Wide World

As your baby hits the nine-month mark or so, the outside world becomes a fascinating place: trees rustling, branches swaying, the sound of birds. You'll get to a point when your baby will want to be turned around in the stroller. You'll know it because he'll start to protest being placed in it. Don't take it personally. Your baby has looked at your face six million times and loves you but now wants to see the world beyond Mommy.

Daniel Pangbourne

CHAPTER 7

Nine to Twelve Months

PARENTS' JOURNEY

You're much more of a relaxed mom and dad now, right? You know your child well, and your child knows you. At this stage, he's probably just saying a few words, but his body language and facial expressions speak volumes, and you know exactly what he's communicating. Plus you have a mental log of what works and what your child needs. All of this put together is making life so much easier, right?

For example, you may be sitting with a friend and your baby is in the stroller kicking her feet and laughing. Then you see a little bit of anxiousness and her facial expression changes. Being able to read her body language plus recognizing that she's been sitting there for twenty minutes while you've been talking allows you to make a very clear decision about what to do next: out for a bit of attention and then down for a nap.

Whereas before you might panic because of your lack of experience and run to him at every little whimper and cry, now you know that you can wait a bit and it's not going to hurt your baby. In fact, it helps teach him eventual patience. This is an important learning for parents and baby: that you're not completely at their beck and call immediately. This is especially critical for parents who have older children, because you are going to need to find that balance as this baby comes into the toddler years while you're also looking after your older children at the same time.

You've done a good job of reading and following my advice. Now, rather than following the text to a T, you're starting to ad-lib based on knowing your baby better than anyone else. That makes sense. You have your way, and other parents have theirs. That's okay. Don't let competitive parents who seek to be right cause you to doubt yourself.

You should be very, very proud of yourselves. Parenting is a very rewarding job, but the rewards are not given through raises or promotions. Hopefully, your family and friends have been telling you how well you've been doing and have continued to be supportive.

Think of all you've given your baby. You may not have the 300-thread-count baby sheets or the latest toys. But your baby has a relaxed, energized parent because you have a consistent sleep routine. Your baby has great social skills because you've been an interactive mother who has made the effort to meet up with other moms and babies. And your baby has confident parents that he trusts.

Make sure that your life is not all about the baby. You may look at him and see that he's very happy and content. But how about you? It's important to focus on yourself too, because your baby's not there to fill a void in your own life. Your baby's there because the pair of you decided to raise a human being in this lifetime.

What things are you doing for yourself? Be sure you have goals for yourself, even if it's just going to the gym twice a week or meeting up with a friend for lunch or doing some work that you have been wanting to do. Recognize that now's the time to start learning to juggle raising your child with other things that are important to you. I disagree with that old saying that once we have kids, our lives stop. Your priorities change, of course, and there are certain things that you don't do anymore. But your life goes on.

Some moms, for instance, put their child into a gym nursery and go swimming before taking their babies to a swim class. This allows them to have some exercise and to release stress, as well as to have fun with their baby afterward. Also, the good thing about leaving your child in the nursery is that it gives her a chance to interact with other children as well as adults other than yourself. It helps her social development and object permanence (the object being you—you go, and come back). It's healthy for her, it's healthy for you, and it's only an hour at the most. Plus, if your child is really crying, the staff can get hold of you in a heartbeat.

New Roles

By this stage, you're leading by example, whether you realize it or not. Your baby is now watching and learning from your every move: how you sit and eat, how you react to situations, your body language. This watching and imitating will go on for years. He's increasingly more aware of the environment, which includes people and feelings, but also sounds and sights. As adults, we take these things for granted, but for babies at this age, they can be terrifying. Your job is to reassure and help him make sense of the world.

A little girl I looked after would freak out every time I pulled the plug out of the bath because of the noise the water made as it gurgled down the hole. So I told her in a sweet tone that that's where the little people live, and the water goes down to make sure that they have their baths too. The thought of these little people made it okay. Not that, being so young, she fully understood me, but my calm voice let her know that everything was all right.

So it's your job to become aware of what might be frightening your baby and reassure her. Airplane noises, fireworks, toilets flushing. Your baby is becoming consciously aware of these now. How you deal with it is important. My advice: validate what she's going through and pacify, but also give a very short and simple reassurance.

Your baby's mobility again accelerates during this period. Babies can think ahead a bit now, but not about the end result. So it's still a time of being on your feet and rescuing him a lot.

It's also the time for a whole new parenting skill: watching your child bump into things when crawling and falling down as he learn to walks. You wish the whole world were made out of rubber, so he'd bounce back without a scratch. You don't want him to fall and hurt himself. But you know that you have to let him experiment to grow.

You need to learn to step back, because your fear and upset are contagious. Over and over I've seen kids fall because their parents yell out, "Watch out." Or fall and be fine until they see a parent upset. Then the wailing starts. This is not to say that you shouldn't validate that your baby's fallen over. But do it in a calm manner.

Indeed, this is a time when you need all of the calm you can muster, because babies at this age do fall and get big bruises. And then you're sitting there worrying what other people are going to think about you as a parent.

That's a place where you don't want to go. Just deal with what you need to deal with, your own family, your own baby. Try not to let your concerns about what other people might think influence the decisions you make for your child. That's what being a confident parent is about—standing in your own belief in yourself.

The Emotions of Weaning

You may have done it sooner, but at some point around now you're probably going to wean your baby. From an emotional point of view, some women can feel very sad about the end of this intimate connection. So don't do it until you're ready.

One thing that helps is to recognize that by weaning, you're taking your bond to a different level, where you still have intimacy with your child. You can still have quiet times, those times when it's just you and her. She's still dependent on you, it's just not about your breasts (if you've got any left, looking at those chicken fillets that you're going to have to put in your bra). Your baby will always be your baby, but now she's heading toward toddlerhood. Your focus here should be on continuing to do your best as a parent to help your child reach her healthy milestones.

I recently helped a woman with this situation with her fourteen-month-old and it was completely liberating for her and her child. She hadn't wanted to give up breast-feeding because it helped her maintain her lack of intimacy with her husband. Now that's changed too.

DEVELOPMENTAL OVERVIEW

Physical

By ten months, she knows her own name, responding by turning her head, moving toward you, or making sounds. She's become a master copycat, mimicking the gestures of those around her. She has become capable of a sequence of actions; for instance, picking up a clothespin and putting it into a pail, then taking it out again.

By the eleventh month, he'll probably be able to "couch walk"—walk while holding onto furniture. Around now, he'll also stand on his own and then take his first step or two without holding on, which will result, no doubt, in great parental delight and applause, which encourages him to keep on trying. You'll find yourself saying "no" more often as you pull him away from potentially dangerous or messy situations and physically remove him to safety.

Around twelve months, she also begins to understand the names of body parts (especially if you name them when you bathe or change her). By one year, she may under-stand up to 100 words, although she may not say more than a few words at this point, or none at all. As long as she is making sounds that have variety of pitch and intensity, you can be sure her first words aren't far away. Feeding herself becomes easier, including drinking from a sippy cup and getting that spoon into her mouth.

By your baby's first birthday, he's typically tripled his birth weight and is 28–32 inches tall. (But remember, it's your baby's growth rate that's important, not these specific numbers.) She'll be able to stack blocks, put things inside of others (nesting containers), and even do one-piece puzzles (those that have big knobs on them are good for helping develop the "pincer" grip, which is the ability to grasp something with thumb and forefinger). She'll also be able to eat with her fingers and "help" you dress her by putting out an arm or leg.

Social/Emotional

During this time, she starts to look to you for what to do when she's unsure. She wants you to indicate with a smile, a word, or a nod that what she's doing is okay. That shows she's developing both self-consciousness and the awareness of social approval and disapproval.

He most likely will cry when you leave, and will show a preference for particular toys. At some point, she figures out that the baby in the mirror is herself.

NEED TO KNOW

WHEN TO CALL THE DOCTOR

- Doesn't crawl by twelve months
- Can't stand when supported by ten months
- Says no single words like *mama* by twelve months
- Does not look for objects that you hide while she watches
- Doesn't use gestures, like shaking head or waving, by twelve months

By the eleventh month, she may begin to exhibit parallel play, meaning playing next to, but not with, another child. She may all of a sudden become afraid of certain objects or sounds, like thunder or the vacuum cleaner. If you can't prevent it—like thunder—comfort her and stay as calm as you can. Your emotions are contagious.

His sense of humor really kicks in now. He knows what makes you laugh, and you'll have a lot of fun together. The downside is that he's going to be testing the boundaries, but not in a way where he's being defiant. It comes from being curious. If he's doing something he shouldn't, you need to begin to establish boundaries through a low tone of voice and a facial expression that shows you're not happy.

You'll begin to see just what a little actor you have given birth to. There should be a baby Oscar night with regards to how babies try and trick us with little coughing noises and head-shaking. Most parents are quite surprised when I tell them that their baby is trying to pull a fast one. "I never knew babies were that clever!" Oh, yeah—believe.

A classic example is when you give her something to eat she doesn't like, and she makes a kind of sound like a throttle of a car trying to start, making out that the food is choking her. Of course, you need to check to see if she is choking, but usually it's only because she doesn't want that particular food. It's a response to change. Like adults, most babies want to stick to what they know and some are more reluctant to experience something new than others.

You'll find her emotions are all over the place during this stage. She's high one moment, then the next moment bursts into tears. And this all happens very quickly.

He also will begin to display separation anxiety, meaning he has figured out that there is only one of you, and he wants you all the time! Babies have no sense of time, so when you leave, they have no idea of when you might be back. Separation anxiety usually begins at ten months and appears again at about eighteen months.

By twelve months, he'll be able to express love to people and objects, with kisses and sounds that indicate affection.

As he hits the one-year milestone, he'll want to begin to do things for himself: feed himself or put things in a shape sorter. The more you can allow him to help, the more his abilities and patience will grow.

THE LEAVE-TAKING TECHNIQUE

NEED TO KNOW

As separation anxiety sets in, it can be extremely upsetting when your baby begins to wail and cling when you try to leave. You may feel guilty, or you can feel suffocated by his constant clinging, wishing he would just leave you alone! Remember that this phase will end, and try to make your leave-takings as calm as possible. Here's an effective leave-taking technique:

- Practice by telling her you're going in another room and will be back in one minute. Then go for a minute and return. She'll learn that you do return.
- Separations are the hardest when your baby is hungry, tired, or sick. As much as possible, leave after he's been fed and had a nap, and, if possible, avoid separations when he's sick.
- Have the other caretaker create a distraction with a toy or bath, etc. Say bye-bye and leave calmly: "Mommy's going now."
- If you're taking her somewhere else to stay—someone's house, a day care center—stay for a few minutes before announcing you're leaving and will be back soon. Then give her a cuddle and go.
- Above all, remember that the wails subside as soon as you leave. They are his attempt to get you to stay. Once that fails, he'll soon get involved with the caretaker.

BABYPROOFING

The goal of this time when it comes to babyproofing is to make sure your baby is safe but free to explore. Check on locks on cabinets and doors. Tack down loose rugs so that your soon-to-be walker won't slip or trip.

In the kitchen, make sure there are no chairs or step stools near the stove that she can climb up on. For food safety, see the section on Feeding in 6–9 months.

Make sure your yard is safe. To avoid a drowning hazard, empty paddling pools after every use (your baby has probably peed in there anyway) and store upside down. If you have a swimming pool, it must have an electric cover or a self-closing and self-locking fence or other safety device to prevent accidental drowning.

Make sure the sandbox has a cover to keep cats out. Get rid of poisonous plants, or teach your baby to avoid them. Make sure playground equipment is anchored properly and meets safety standards. Never mow the lawn, use a weed whacker, or barbecue when your baby's outside.

SETTING FIRM GROUND

Cornerstone Routine

Here's a whole routine put together: food, sleep, stimulations. I've done the first one to give you the idea. Fill in the second with your actual times and activities. Be sure to see my feeding schedule for more detail on the food portion, as well as the weaning schedule.

CORNERSTONE SCHEDULE: 9–12 MONTHS	
Time	Activity
morning	breakfast, bottle
	play
mid-morning	nap
noon	lunch
12:30 PM	play
mid-afternoon	nap
late afternoon	dinner
early evening	play/bathtime
evening	bedtime

(continued on next page)

CORNERSTONE SCHEDULE: 9–12 MONTHS	
Time	*Activity*
_____	breakfast, bottle
_____	play
_____	nap
_____	lunch
_____	play
_____	nap
_____	dinner
_____	play/bathtime
_____	bedtime

Sleep

One of the biggest mistakes people make is when their baby learns how to climb out of her crib. They say to one another, "Oh, it's time to put her in a big bed." No, it's not. It's time for you teach your baby how to *stay in her crib.* She's not ready for a big bed. Place her in the crib without toys except for one cuddly. When she climbs out, put her back and say, "Stay in your crib and sleep." If she cries, use the controlled crying technique again.

By now you've got a solid sleep schedule of an AM and PM nap and a full night's sleep. Here are two possible routines. Be aware that your baby will test boundaries around sleep between 8–13 months. You may have to use the controlled crying technique.

	SLEEP ROUTINE: 9–12 MONTHS
	No catnap before bedtime. Otherwise it will be hard for your baby to sleep. If he takes a catnap, you have to push back bedtime by thirty minutes to one hour.

Time	Activity
_____	play
_____	mid-morning nap (1½ **OR** 2 hours)
_____	play
_____	afternoon nap (2 hours)
_____	play
_____	bedtime (10–12 hours)

Getting Off the Pacifier

As I mentioned earlier, for a variety of reasons, I think babies should be weaned off their pacifiers by around age one for daytime, eighteen months for sleeping. If you've only used it as a sleep aid, that won't be so difficult.

By now he's settled into a good sleep pattern and has the ability to go to sleep on his own. Begin by putting him down for naps without the pacifier. After a few days of that, don't give it in the evening either. Here's a great chance to introduce a bedtime story and a cuddly stuffed toy to the routine. Tuck him in with his cuddly and say, "night-night." Gone with the pacifier.

If your baby has been using the pacifier during the daytime as well, as soon as they've started to make words, you want to get rid of it at least during the day so that they're communicating verbally more. Begin by giving it only at night, and then wean that as well, as I suggested previously.

Obviously it's a different story when we're talking about babies who suck their fingers or thumbs. Normally the child who has a pacifier is the child who doesn't suck her thumb. If your baby intensely sucks fingers or thumb then obviously it wrinkles all up like a prune. At this point, it's best just to ignore such behavior. If you see chafing, make sure to apply lotion to prevent cracking.

Setting Boundaries

Your little one is far too young to understand right from wrong or complicated reasons why he shouldn't crawl out the window. So you should never try to reason with a baby. And you should never spank a child!

But you can begin to teach him boundaries through your tone of voice. This is not permission to yell. Rather, to indicate disapproval, state firmly in a low tone: "No, we don't smear food on the cat" and then remove him from the temptation. And don't forget to keep praising everything done right!

FEEDING

As she approaches one year, you can introduce a variety of different foods. Make a food plan that is balanced and nutritious.

By one, he should be able to use a spoon to dig out what he wants. He'll eat with his fingers mostly, so be prepared for mealtimes to be a slow, messy, fun process. Feeding himself helps his fine motor coordination and pincer grip, and the more he practices getting spoon and hand to mouth, the better he'll get. Yogurt is good for practicing because it stays on the spoon well. You're there at this point to provide appropriate foods in appropriate-sized pieces, to watch for choking, to help when needed, and to clean up afterward.

Babies at this age will try anything, so start teaching good eating habits and proper portion sizes through your choices. Get clued up, buy books, read up. Obesity and type 2 diabetes are on the rise. Do your part in curbing these epidemics!

FOOD TRICKS

One way to help him learn to use a spoon and eat unfamiliar things is to put a bit of new food in yogurt. Make each spoonful less yogurt and more of the savory food, until he's got it.

I am a believer in babies being strapped into their high chairs to eat meals on a schedule as I described previously. That helps them establish healthy habits of mindful eating as they grow, rather than turning into mindless 24-7 grazers. It's your moral responsibility to provide your child healthy, balanced meals. The more she learns to eat right now, the more she's likely to do so into adulthood.

FEEDING SCHEDULE: 9–12 MONTHS

Here I've given routines for two bottles and for three.

Time	Activity
6:30 AM	breast-feed 20–40 minutes or bottle-feed 8 oz.
8:30 AM	breakfast
11:00 AM	snack/fruit
1:00 PM	lunch
3:30 PM	snack
5:00 PM	dinner
6:30 PM	breast-feed 20–40 minutes or bottle-feed 8–9 oz.
7:00 AM	breast-feed 20–40 minutes or bottle-feed 8–9 oz.
9:00 AM	breakfast
10:30 AM	snack
12:00–1:00 PM	lunch
3:30 PM	fruit
4:30 PM	dinner
6:30 PM	breast-feed 20–40 minutes or bottle-feed 8–9 oz.
7:00 AM	breast-feed 20–40 minutes or bottle-feed 8–9 oz.
9:30 AM	breakfast
12:30 PM	lunch/dessert
3:30 PM	breast-feed 20–40 minutes or bottle-feed 6 oz.
5:30 PM	dinner
7:00 PM	breast-feed 20–40 minutes or bottle-feed 8 oz.

Weaning From the Breast

The most common time period for breast-feeding is one year. But if you want to do it beyond then, that's your choice. Emotionally, Mom needs to be ready. If you're not, question whether your reactions are healthy and in the interest of the baby. There's a point when I see a toddler walking over to the breast and I know that he's using the breast as a pacifier. There is a point where instead of nurturance and bonding, there a complacency between the baby and the mother, where she becomes just a milking machine. Then it's time to cut it off, as there is nothing to be gained here that's a healthy progression.

If your baby is eating solids regularly and getting fluids from a cup or bottle and you want to stop breast-feeding, cut the feeds down to one in the AM and one in the PM, if it isn't already occurring. Then skip the AM feed and don't offer the breast again till the PM. If you taper off, you'll find your milk supply dwindling as well.

If your baby stops abruptly, you may go through a painful period where your breasts are engorged. Don't pump to relieve the pressure, as this will just keep your milk supply going. Wear a nursing bra until the pain subsides. You can also use ice packs or bags of frozen peas covered in a dish towel on your breasts to reduce pain. In a few days, the milk production will stop and the pain will disappear.

Weaning from the Bottle

Bottle-fed babies should also be weaned at around a year to reduce the possibility of iron deficiency due to not eating enough iron-rich foods. This process should begin with weaning from powdered formula to cow's milk. Over several weeks, lower the formula and up the cow's milk in his bottles. Here's a chart to show you how:

Week 1:	6 oz. formula, 2 oz. cow's milk
Week 2:	5 oz. formula, 3 oz. cow's milk
Week 3:	4 oz. formula, 4 oz. cow's milk
Week 4:	3 oz. formula, 5 oz. cow's milk
Week 5:	2 oz. formula, 6 oz. cow's milk
Week 6:	1 oz. formula, 7 oz. cow's milk
Week 7:	all cow's milk

Once he's drinking all cow's milk, he's probably ready to graduate to a sippy cup. You're about to be bottle free!

Weaning on to a Sippy Cup

Around the one-year mark, you want to wean off bottle or breast to a sippy cup, making sure, of course, that your child still gets their daily intake of milk, which by now should be 16 oz. Here are three routines to show you how it can work:

OPTION 1:	
morning	breakfast, milk in sippy cup and in food
noon	lunch/dessert
mid-afternoon	snack, sippy cup
evening	dinner
OPTION 2:	
morning	breakfast, milk in sippy cup
mid-morning	snack
noon	lunch
mid-afternoon	snack
evening	dinner, milk in sippy cup
OPTION 3:	
morning	breakfast, milk in sippy cup
mid-morning	snack
noon	lunch
mid-afternoon	snack
evening	dinner/dessert, milk in sippy cup or bottle

PARENTCRAFT

Holding and Carrying

Even when she's this age, you still want to be spending lots of time holding your little one close to you. Most of those "special moments" are right there in the middle of silence, just the two of you as she puts her little fingers on your face or presses gently on your eyelids, exploring the features of your face.

Around nine months, your baby might express a preference of who she wants to be held by. Normally, it is the person she spends the most time with. If this is you, Mom, make a point of not being available sometimes so that your partner gets a chance to continue to develop a bond too. For the sake of some parents who don't want to admit it openly, I have something to say: You may like the fact that your baby is crying for you and not your partner because it flatters your ego, and he may say he doesn't mind. But please, put the shoe on the other foot and understand what it must feel like. As a parent you can't help but take it personally. So do what you can to make sure your baby stretches out his arms for both of you.

Bathing

When they're this age, I like to have fun while washing babies' hair. I stick a play mirror on the tiles of the bathtub so they can see their hair sticking up like a Mohawk or slicked back. It's all about creating fun together. But only if your baby has lots of hair. Some are still quite minimal in their locks.

By a year, if he walks early, he'll most likely want to start standing up in the bath. So be very careful. It doesn't take much for a baby to slip and bang his head. Hang on at all times! Seated is best.

Dressing

This may be a time when dressing or undressing can be quite difficult because your baby refuses to let you change him. Again, we're looking at distraction. When your baby can stand, or is pulling himself up on furniture, lay him down to get his diaper on, then let him stand up to get dressed while you're sitting down. He can lean on your shoulders while you pull up his trousers. Then have him sit down while you put on his shirt. Then pull him up again to lean on you while you snap the snaps. He'll actually find this fun because he's quite pleased with himself being able to stand and get dressed. And all the ups and downs will keep him stimulated.

From this time frame on, I love using soft-soled, suede, corduroy, or leather booties. They're something you can put over an outfit.

First Shoes for the Early Walkers

Once your baby becomes a walker, which is usually 6–8 weeks after she's consistently and confidently walking around, it's time for shoes. You'll know this because the toes will be flat on the floor, which you can encourage by taking her socks off so that she can get better balance. This is quite an exciting time because it's another milestone. A lot of people save their baby's first shoes as a memento, and some even get them bronzed.

Because your baby is so young and won't be able to undo her own shoes, it doesn't really matter whether they're buckle or Velcro, although Velcro is easier for you.

Go to a shop that provides fittings for both length and width. Shoes should have about a half-inch inch of room beyond the toe, be wide enough for all toes to lie flat, and the heel should not ride up. Avoid plastic shoes because they don't allow feet to breathe.

Lots of brands cater to new walkers. First shoes should be very light, with a lightweight rubber sole so your child is able to lift up her foot. If the shoe is too heavy, your baby won't be able to lift her foot but will clump around like Frankenstein.

These are not cheap, the official first pair of shoes! However, it's essential that you get good quality shoes from her first walking pair throughout toddlerhood and beyond. You've got to remember that even though your baby's walking, her foot is still young. The bones are still soft, so it's incredibly important for that first shoe to be right. Too many parents look for fashion instead of looking out for their children's feet. Choose a proper shoe over fashion.

Doctor Visits

Of course you've been to the doctor with your baby for his regular checkups and if he caught an infection. But now your child's a lot bigger, moving around more, and most likely experiencing, "This is a new place. I don't remember here." So going to the doctor for the one-year checkup is another scenario you need to plan for.

Make sure you take his diaper bag with a few things that will keep him occupied. And if an injection is needed, it's always better to have your child sitting on your lap facing you so that you've got eye contact and you're talking to him, with your arm around his shoulders and upper torso and his legs straight across your lap. This allows the doctor or nurse to give the injection in the thigh, which is the meatiest area.

TAKING TEMPERATURE

From nine months onward, you can take your baby's temperature by placing a digital thermometer under her arm as well as taking it rectally. This can be a godsend as she may now be quite strong in protesting the anal one. Be sure to read your thermometer's instructions because how long you hold it there and what reading is normal varies.

STIMULATION AND EXPLORATIONS

By this point, your baby is moving around and exploring more. She may be holding onto knobs of lower cupboards and coffee table edges. She may even have started to use a few words. Whether she's speaking or not, her communication capacity is a lot stronger. She makes it as clear as possible by pointing. In this period, you're concentrating even more on crawling, climbing, and pulling himself up games.

Because separation and stranger anxiety are strong now, you want to engage her in activities that will engross her as a way to distract from anxiety. At about one, she may begin to form attachment to a soft animal, blankie, or other cuddly toy. These are great anxiety reducers.

Remember to keep on giving solo playtime. By one year, you're looking at her spending ten minutes engaged in an activity that she really enjoys.

Talking for Two

This age can be frustrating for little ones because their minds sort of know what they want to say, but verbally they're not there. So your job is to turn everything into a question and then answer it yourself, to help him link actions with words. Double up on everything you say: "Do you want your hat? Would you like your hat? Do you want me to give it to you? Here it is." You may end up feeling like a parrot talking to yourself, but it's all part of being a parent: proposing questions and answering them to teach him how to respond to what you're saying.

Even though you'll be encouraging your child to talk more and offering her choices—"Do you want the red one or the blue one?"—she's not going to actually turn around and say, "I'll take the red one." She may just take one from the two you offer. But the more you talk, the more she's going to understand. By the age of about thirteen or fourteen months, babies grasp exactly what you're saying even though they can't communicate back fully.

When he speaks his first words, they may not be accurate—*ba-ba* for "bottle," for instance. Be sure you respond as if it were correct, but use the correct word in response: "Here's your bottle, darling." In this way, he'll learn the correct word more easily.

If you speak more than one language at home, great! She'll learn both. But my advice is to keep them separated, Mom with one, Dad with the other. I've found you compromise basic English by trying to teach three or four.

Pincer Play

This is a time to really help your baby with her pincer grip—using the thumb and forefinger together. Wooden puzzles with the little knobs are great for this. So are stacking cups, blocks, or plastic rings on a stick. If you don't have a ring, you can take a paper towel tube and have your baby put plain bangles on it, supervised of course.

Climb, Tunnel, and Hide

This is a great time to find an activity class. You're developing his social skills and supporting movement and coordination by having him crawl in tunnels, over big foam blocks, and under parachutes.

Stairs are what your child will want to climb, so make sure it's always supervised. Make sure stair gates are closed. Teach her to come down by letting her back up and reverse, then take it one leg at a time with you behind. Also walking in and out of little tents and hideouts built under tables and chairs makes for much fun.

Push Toys

I like push toys with activity boards on them for this age because you get two for one. Of course, they only work if your baby is walking.

Musical Instruments

Music is incredibly important, and something that I use consistently, beginning with newborns to soothe them. At this age, it's great to give your baby some maracas or a tambourine, triangle, or little drum. It will bring her hours of fun. It allows her to not only make music, but to grasp rhythm as she moves her body to the beat. Her little personality shines out. There are lots of different types— leather, metal, plastic—you decide.

You don't even need to buy instruments. I like to get lots of different dried beans like lentils and garbanzos and place them in different sizes of plastic containers with sturdy lids. Your baby can grasp and shake them to hear the different noises. Again, be sure you supervise, as it is dangerous for a baby to eat the beans.

Water, Water, Everywhere

Babies of this age typically love water, whether in the bath or in a bowl. They love getting their hands wet and being able to put things in water and splash around. Yes, it may be messy but find a time in the day for water play. Lay down towels if need be, and do it with them, for both safety and fun.

Big Motion Games

This is the time for big motion games, like flying airplane, bouncing on your knee, being swung under the armpits (never by the hands—you can dislocate a shoulder or break an arm that way).

Those little red Radio Flyers are great to pull little ones in. Or you can use a big cardboard box or a plastic laundry basket to push or tie a rope on, and pull indoors or out. I spent a lot of time doing this with babies this age, and they went through their toddler years enjoying it too. It's great to use sound as well: *Vroom, vroom, vroom,* you're a car; *clickety-clack,* you're a train; and *chug, chug,* you're a boat.

Don't be afraid to take your baby at this stage to the playground and put him in the baby swing and gently go back and forth. This is also the time you can lift him lightly up into the air and catch him, or place him on a roll tube or large ball and move him from side to side or back and forth. All these are games that allow you not only to connect physically, but reinforce the trust between you.

Where's the . . .

Now's the time to start playing visual memory games. You can show him a simple board book picture and ask, "Where's the duck? There's the duck. What does the duck say? Quack!" By around twelve months, he'll start to associate the name with the picture, as well as what sound it makes. It's all setting the groundwork for when he's a few months older and surprises you by saying, "Quack, quack."

THE YEAR MILESTONE

There's no doubt that every parent says it: "My God, that year went too quickly. Where did the time go?" While you're going through it, the time was passing. And then suddenly his first birthday's here, you've got the few friends around the birthday cake, all the babies are crying because the noise from singing "Happy Birthday" is all too much, and you're sitting there crying, "I can't believe it happened so quickly!" Your baby changed from a newborn to a one-year-old who's talking in one-syllable words and piling that cake into his mouth.

Then you recognize how much you've matured. Okay, so you don't look like you did in your wedding photos. But you've also gained something precious: a maturity and confidence you didn't have before. As much as you listen to other people's opinions and take advice from experts, you trust yourself a lot more. You're able to recognize that inner voice, your intuition, and pay attention to it.

You feel proud that you can hold your head up high and join the ranks of experienced parents. You are grateful for all you've learned this year, and for the beautiful child before you still in one piece. You realize he's his own person and not just an extension of the two of you.

Congratulations! You've done your first year! Now, ready or not, it's toddler time. But you *are* ready—you know you are—and that's the difference. A year ago, you weren't sure.

PART III

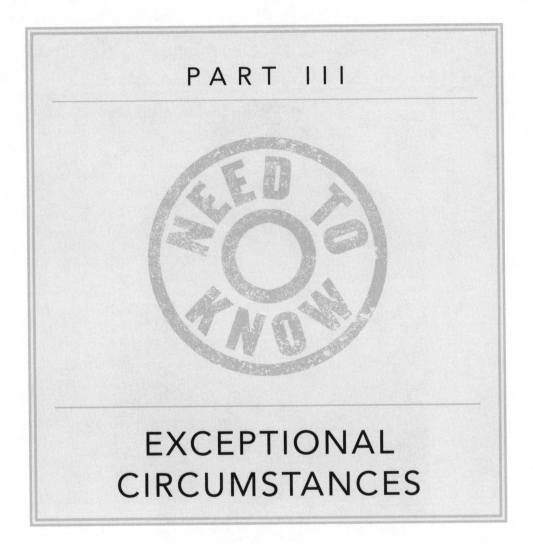

EXCEPTIONAL CIRCUMSTANCES

CHAPTER 8

Multiple Births

ell . . . congratulations! You're the parents of more than one bundle of joy! And you're in good company—there are more than 130,000 multiple births a year in the U.S., mostly as a result of fertility treatments. And because of ultrasound, unlike in the past, the fact that there's more than one will not be sprung on you at the hospital. You have time to prepare, which is good news. Needless to say, you'll have more than a handful! Get as much rest as possible before the birth so you'll have as much energy as possible. I know you'll find that multiples are a real blessing, and this book will help you feel at ease throughout this first year.

As a nanny, I've looked after twins. In fact, the job I had just before I started *Supernanny* was looking after twin girls. Multiples still hold fascination with people. They'll stop you in the street and ask, "Who was born first? Who's the oldest?" "Oh, they are adorable!"

Because of IVF and other fertility treatments, many parents of multiples are older. And these parents tell me that it takes very little to wear them out, and they think it's because of their age. I always say, how do you know? If you're in this situation, it's true that you may not have the same kind of stamina you had when you were in your twenties. But you have something else: maturity, stability, and patience, the things that people learn along the way as they grow older. Those qualities will help you make this year a joyful experience.

No matter your age, let me reassure you about one thing: I can definitely say

189

from experience that things get easier after nine months on every level. Once your babies are older and you can turn them toward one another in their bouncy seats, they'll amuse each other. There is something really special about the relationship between multiples, whether identical or not. A wonderful connection with each other that is a joy not only for them, but for you.

For the most part, the first year for parents of multiples is the same as for one, except you're multiplying it all—multiplying the joy, multiplying the juggling, multiplying the need for a routine, and the need for help. In this chapter, I will highlight those things you need to consider in addition to what I've written in the rest of the book as a result of your unique circumstance. If your multiples were born early or are smaller than average, please also read Chapter 9 on preemies.

Equipment

Your decision process of equipping a nursery may be different as you must consider money, space, and the practicality of the situation of more than one. Obviously you're going to need more equipment. But that doesn't mean you need double or triple of everything. Don't buy more than necessary. There's only a certain period of time you're going to use this equipment, and then you're not going to need it anymore. You're certainly not going to be thinking about needing it again for a while after just giving birth to two or three kids, that's for sure! So, it'd be up under wraps in the attic until then.

For instance, two car seats are of course essential. But you only need one diaper pail. You can only change one child at a time, so one changing mat is fine unless you plan to use two for double baby massage. Bottle-fed babies typically go through eight bottles or so a day, so depending on how many you have, you're going to need more bottles. But you don't need double or triple, if you sterilize more often.

I would definitely recommend each baby having his own bassinet and crib. Many parents think that because multiples have grown together in the womb, they would be better off sleeping together. I disagree because there's always one baby more dominant. Just when you've gotten them off to sleep, the most dominant will make noise and will wake up the other(s). If they sleep separately, each has the chance to get the sleep they need. More importantly, some research has indicated that sleeping together may increase the risk of SIDS. Since being a multiple is itself a risk factor for SIDS, I strongly urge you to put your babies to sleep by themselves on their backs. All swaddled nicely.

For triplets, I like the strollers that have one seat behind the other rather than side by side. They're long, but not wide so they fit through the doorways of shops. I call them stretch limos. The side-by-side strollers are great if you want to go jogging. Nobody's going to get in your way, are they? You feel like you're driving one of those military tanks. Nobody messes with you when you're on the curb, here you come! Shop doors have been getting wider and automatic, making it more possible to fit in. I think they've realized that if you can't get in, you won't be buying anything. In other words, no mommies shopping on impulse! If you opt for a side-by-side stroller, be sure it has one long footrest rather than two, because babies' feet can get caught in the gap.

Individual slings, seats, swings, and bouncy chairs will come in incredibly handy and enable you to get things done more easily. Plus, it allows your babies to do things together, which is part of the fun of your unique situation—although don't put one baby in front and one in back in one, please.

When it comes to toys and clothes, I don't believe that you should buy two (or three, four) of everything. Some things you will, and some things you won't. You'll find your way with this. It's nice for them to have some things the same and some different. And when there's only one of something, it will help them learn to share. In the long run, group activities are nice if they all have balls and rattles. But, for instance, they can all babble in a baby ring together.

Look ahead and stock up. Have a couple of spare cases of diapers and formula so you're not stuck in the middle of the night saying, "Achh! I've run out!" Don't buy like a hurricane's coming, but definitely have a little bit extra just in case. Each time you go shopping, buy one extra thing, especially at the two-for-the-price-of-one specials. It's a way of creating an emergency supply without creating a big dent in your pocket.

PARENTS' JOURNEY

From the beginning, you will start to recognize how very different each of your babies are as little human beings. Each has her own temperament and personality. Be sure you identify those differences as strengths, and don't compare one to the other in a negative way. You will find that they complement one another. You need to be able to give each what she needs emotionally and developmentally. With the help of your partner, friends, and family, be sure to spend some time alone with each, even just for a little while. It will allow you to really identify their little personalities and temperaments, which can sometimes fall to the sideline as you've been so busy just trying to constantly keep track of it all 24-7.

Be honest with yourselves about the toll on the two of you, because dealing with two or more is very demanding. Keep talking about how you can support one another so that each partner doesn't always feel overwhelmed. Remember, it's the two of you raising the babies together. And if you have other children, it can feel like you're running your own day care center. I know a family that has two sets of twins plus an older child. With minimum help, they've done quite fine, and so will you.

Especially at the very beginning, you'll want to have at least one or two more pairs of hands. A mother's helper is really good. Or a nanny, doula, or relative, any kind of additional supportive help. The more assistance you can get, the easier it will feel. Check out the resource guide in the back.

Becoming overloaded with everyday needs can leave you forgetting about yourselves too. Be kind to yourself, please. When you feel brave enough, take that step and book a date night, even if it's a quick meal out. Of course most parents of multis under nine months old would rather chill on the sofa with takeout. Do that too. I've babysat while parents were in the living room taking a few hours off.

It also helps to meet with other parents in your circumstances. There are also wonderful groups of parents of multiples you can join as well as special Web sites that can offer emotional and practical support. See the resource guide.

However many children you're juggling, be aware that everything will take more time: time to get everyone out the door, time to feed everyone, and so on. You're running a production line—multiple bottles, baby food, laundry. The more kids you have, the more organized you need to be. As the babies get older, it will all take less time.

Work out your priorities, what you can and can't let go of. Do you need to wash every day, or can it be every other day? Is it essential that the TV gets wiped over every day? Or can it go for a week? If you can afford it, get a cleaning person in. I know many women who feel so proud to say, "I do my own cleaning." Swallow your pride. No polishing the martyr crown!

There's a lot of fun to be had with multiples. You'll find yourself in total amazement that these babies are yours. You'll have days where everybody is cooing over your babies, how beautiful they are, and how they should be in baby modeling school. These moments compensate for the times that you're up at 3:00 in the morning thinking, "Oh my God, there's two (or three or four) of them! Well, they always say be careful of what you wish for."

I'm not going to harp about how tired you'll be, because you know this already. It is to be expected. You're human, not a robot.

But I want to emphasize again having an upbeat mentality. You can create a lifestyle that works for you and your new family. Expect the smooth as well as the rough, the positives as well as the negatives. Focus on what you want, not on what you don't. Have a positive mind-set so you can enjoy parenting these amazing children of yours. So that you can enjoy this new stage of your lives and be proud, confident parents.

I've very much enjoyed looking after twins. Very much. I believe it will bring out the best in you. You have to learn to adapt very, very quickly. You think on the fly and learn to multitask very quickly. Pretty soon, you're a seasoned parent of multiples, able not only to adjust to any challenge, but to enjoy yourself in the process!

Oh, and I forgot to mention: eyes do grow faster out of the back of your head . . . or maybe it just seems that way.

DEVELOPMENTAL OVERVIEW

Even if they are visually identical, you will find that each baby develops at his own pace. You may see that one turns over, sits up, or starts to talk sooner than the other. Or one is able to pick up his spoon and feed himself before the other one. This is where, as a parent, you want to be sure to treat each as an individual. That means you see the potential in the one who's ahead and build on that, while encouraging the other as well. You may even find that the one who talks earlier ends up at about eighteen months doing the talking for both of them. So make sure you encourage each at whatever rate.

You need to be aware of the differences and respond to each baby, without getting frustrated or fearful about the differences. This is no different from what you would do if you had one baby who was developing at a different pace from a friend's baby. Check with your doctor if you're truly concerned.

You may find that your babies have different tastes in food as well. Or one may eat more than the other. Emotionally, they may respond to things differently. They will each have their own temperament and personality. One child might cry at fireworks, and the other not. I can't tell you how many parents of newborn multiples say to me: "They may have been in the same womb, but they are individuals." And of course that's true. Separate souls, separate hearts. Again, it's your job as parents to enjoy the differences as well as the similarities, and to support each child becoming herself. Different strokes for these little folks, most definitely.

As they get closer to a year, you'll notice that they will begin to pay a lot of attention to one another. Putting them together in a big baby gym is a great way to observe how they interact—touch one another's faces, gurgle and smile together.

From the beginning, multis are used to having another person around 24-7, and their social abilities develop very quickly, as they are able to communicate with another little person about everything all the time. Sometimes I've watched how they make each other laugh with a facial expression or squeal. It's healthy to let them just be together.

The funny thing is that when they reach about a year, you go into neutral and they find their balance with you. *They* find it, not you. They work out their balance with one another and with you.

SETTING FIRM GROUND

In the beginning, parents have great intentions to treat each baby separately when it comes to eating, sleeping, and playing. That all goes out the window after about three weeks, as you realize that the bags under your eyes look like double cheeks. That's why I suggest you feed them at the same time, and then they'll sleep roughly at the same time—for your health and sanity.

Just as you would with a single baby, establish that sleep and feeding routine, so you can manage your time more efficiently. Again, that means flexibility within routine. That's not to say that if you have your twins on an afternoon naptime and one wakes up ten minutes before the other, you'd make that one stay in the crib for ten minutes trying to get him back off to sleep. You get the one who's up earlier. And that may mean that you run ten minutes earlier with feeding that one too. The slight variations in schedules allow you to have one-on-one time with each.

FEEDING

One way to make your life easier while still providing the immunity of breast milk is to pump breast milk and give it in bottles, supplemented by formula if need be. Or breast-feed at home and give them a bottle when you're out and about, because it's easier and you want to make your life as easy as possible. Another benefit of bottles is that you'll know exactly how much each is getting. Of course it's your decision. Some moms of triplets who've chosen to breast-feed have told me that it helps them bond emotionally with each of them.

If you have twins and decide to breast-feed, the best position is shown in the diagram with both babies on *V*-pillows with their legs facing your back. Make sure you're very comfortable because you're going to be there for at least half an hour. Switch which breast each baby suckles so that you don't get flatter if one feeds more than the other. Plus it'll give them a different view! You can burp them at the same time too, by simply turning them over across your lap together.

When they start on solid foods, parents always ask me, which one do I feed first? Just take turns: today I fed you first for breakfast; now I feed you for lunch first. No favorites. They'll learn to take turns very quickly. That's one of the marvelous advantages of having multiples. They learn early about taking turns and sharing. You can line them up in their high chairs and go down the line. Of

course, if you don't have a high chair for each, then they *really* have to take turns. They may not like it, but hey, ho . . .

PARENTCRAFT

One of the facts of having more than one baby is that if you are by yourself with them and changing one, you can't be changing the other. So someone might cry a bit longer. Again, take turns. Make sure that the most dominant one doesn't always come first just because he's making the most noise. Give the one who's waiting a toy to hold onto.

Try not to beat yourself up about not being able to respond instantly. Your children are going to learn a little bit more patience earlier because of their circumstances, and that's very healthy. They won't do everything at the same pace. For instance, one may be slower at eating, so the other will have to wait.

As much as possible, make it easy on yourself by bathing each on alternate days, to lessen the duty. Or do it together and take a day off. Trim their nails at different times depending on the rate of growth.

Divide up the tasks between the two of you parents: laundry duty, cooking, etc. When both of you are there, each of you take primary charge of one baby, alternating so you both get time with each. Or take them both so the other adult gets a real rest. You'll soon see what works best.

With triplets or more, holding and carrying simultaneously is virtually impossible. With twins, it's a bit easier—two hips, two kids. But that will create back problems, so try not to do it.

A quick tip is to always place yourself in the middle so they learn to share you: two legs to sit on, two arms, thank God. Around nine months they will get a little possessive about wanting you to themselves. I would suggest you approach this with "There's room for all of us." Unless it's that special one-on-one time, which is so crucial at this period because almost all their time with you is shared. During this period especially, be sure to find ways of giving them individual attention without the other around.

As much as possible, do all the things you would do with one, like baby massage. With two, put yourself in the middle and one on each side of you on a blanket on the floor. You can stroke each back and tummy at the same time. With more than two, rotate them.

STIMULATION AND EXPLORATIONS

Because multiples develop at different paces, your job as a parent is to provide the stimulation each needs. That may mean moving the more developed one on to more advanced toys or games, because otherwise she'll get bored if you're waiting for the other to catch up. Keep the one moving forward while you're encouraging the other to get to where the first one already is.

When they become mobile, you've really got to be careful. You've got more than one to watch like a hawk. Here's where a playpen can really come in handy. Put them in together for about ten minutes. Then you can grab a bite of lunch or go to the bathroom. But don't overdo it. Using a playpen as a babysitter is neglect.

Enroll them in activities with other babies and see if a relative can come with you or alert the staff that you will need an extra pair of hands at the class. With swimming, you absolutely need one adult for each baby.

If one becomes ill, the other(s) must follow in tow. Your primary job is to get your little one better. (To then find out the other has it the following week, right?)

YOU'RE REALLY EARNING THAT BADGE

When you learn to raise twins, triplets, or quads, at the end of the first year you've passed the parent test blindfolded! That saying "two's company, three's a crowd" is not true in the baby world. It's "two's a pair, three's a party." Olé!

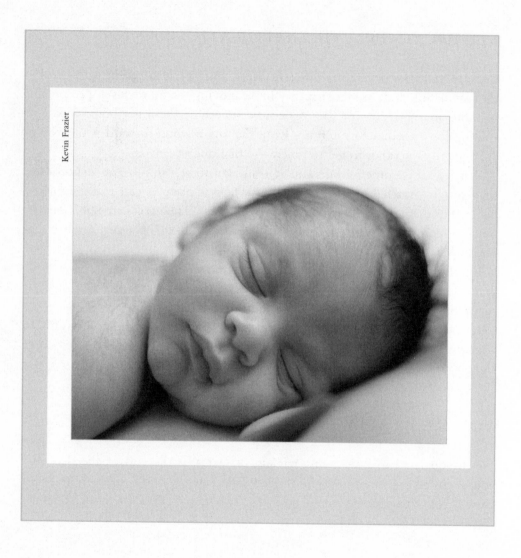

Kevin Frazier

CHAPTER 9

Preemies and
Other Special Needs

ongratulations! Just like every other parent reading this book, you've just given birth to a wonderful new baby. Yours just came a bit early or with a health issue, which means he needs special treatment. I want to encourage you to get all the practical and emotional support you need to feel more at ease for the first year and beyond. There are lots of resources, information, and support available. See the resource guide. I also want to offer my thoughts so that you can be a confident parent and enjoy this first year as much as possible, because like every other parent you deserve to!

In the beginning, all the information you may be bombarded with might not be easy for the two of you to digest. You may be experiencing lots of mixed emotions. Whatever your circumstances and however you may be feeling, I believe every baby is born with a healthy spirit. It will be your job to recognize that beauty beyond the mental or physical realm so that your child will be loved and nurtured without a shadow of a doubt. In the process, you will, as parents, learn to put everything else into perspective.

PREMATURE BABIES:
DEVELOPMENTAL OVERVIEW

Premature babies are born preterm, meaning before their due dates. The longer a baby stays in the womb, the more it can develop. Some babies, even though they may be born 3–4 weeks early, don't seem to be behind developmentally.

Usually, however, if your baby was born prematurely, he's smaller and more fragile than other newborns. The good news is that due to medical advances, even babies born at only twenty-eight weeks have a 95 percent or better chance of survival. He's just going to need special medical care around the clock, especially if he was less than three pounds at birth.

Preemies' weight is measured in grams, and the reason they must be incubated is that they have little or no body fat and so must be kept warm. Often preemies have breathing issues because of immature lung development and may have sleep apnea, meaning they stop breathing while sleeping. They're also more likely to have jaundice, abnormal blood sugar, and hernias. These things clear up with medical attention as they get older.

If they're extremely premature, they may be born covered in down, which will fall out. They may look more wrinkled and fragile, as they have not yet developed muscle on their bones. Depending on how premature they are, they may also have translucent skin, a bald head, sealed-shut eyes, and may not have nipples. Their blood vessels may be visible under their skin. Never fear—as they grow, they will look more and more like the baby you were imagining.

Because development-wise he's not gone full term, you're going to take care of him once he comes home in such a way as to enable him to play catch-up. Generally speaking, he'll be behind the amount of time he was premature. If he was born two months premature, for instance, at four months, he'll probably be at the two-month stage of development. Each baby catches up at his own rate, and usually are age-appropriate by age two or so, although some continue to have a bit of a lag. They often grow in spurts.

Health Issues

Because your baby's immune system is less developed, be sure you check before bringing small children to visit the baby in the hospital. Keeping your baby clear of infection is so important for her health, and catching a cold is twice as harmful as it is with a baby who's fully developed.

At home, you should restrict visitors at least in the beginning, and keep your baby away from crowds. You want to keep a close watch on any fevers and will probably have more regular doctor visits to make sure she's doing okay. Preemies are more at risk for ear and eye infections, and may have hearing problems. If your baby doesn't jump at loud noises, see your doctor.

PARENTS' JOURNEY

Don't be afraid to ask all the questions you need. The staff in the neonatal intensive care unit is trained to help you as well as your baby. Having a premature baby can be very scary for parents, particularly when he's hooked up to all those tubes and monitors in the hospital. You may feel anxious or depressed that you have to go home and leave him there, especially if you have other little ones at home already. See if you can trade off with other family members so that someone is always there, and you get time to recover yourself. Hold her, especially skin to skin, as much as possible. It's good for you and for her.

I've taken care of premature babies and realize that as parents, you have to deal with the feeling that your baby is fragile. It's easy to be concerned, even after she's been approved to leave the hospital and come home. Be aware that your baby's not going to be out of the hospital until the doctor feels that she's safe to be released in good health. If you don't already know it, learning infant CPR can give you greater peace of mind. I strongly recommended it to every parent, not just those with preemies.

Many women feel like it is their fault that their baby was born prematurely. They worry that they caused it somehow: Did they eat something? Do something? Not do something? No one knows for sure why it happens. Try not to blame yourself. It was out of your control.

FEEDING

Because preemies have less fully developed immune systems, you can give your baby a great health boost by breast-feeding if at all possible. However, some babies born prematurely have trouble feeding because they've been born before the sucking reflex develops (that happens somewhere between 32–34 weeks) and aren't able yet to latch on. If this is the case, he will be fed through a tube in the nose in the hospital.

Be sure to have skin-to-skin contact, and have her nuzzle your breast in any case so that she'll be ready to breast-feed when the reflex comes in. Your doctor may suggest vitamins and minerals, especially iron, to supplement breast milk or formula.

Premature babies need to be fed more often than full-term ones: as much as ten feedings a day to prevent dehydration. If she has 6–8 wet diapers a day, you know she's getting enough. She may spit up more, which may interfere with gaining weight. Talk to your doctor if you're concerned.

PARENTCRAFT

Baby Seats

One thing to be aware of with preemies is that research has shown that they can develop breathing problems if left in a seat for long periods of time. Talk to your doctor about this. Keep trips in the car short, and make sure someone is sitting with your baby to check on her breathing when you're driving. It's also recommended that you recline the seat as much as possible while still following the car seat manufacturer's guidelines, and make sure her head and body aren't slumped over. Never leave her alone in the car, and don't put her in a baby seat while in the house. Use the bassinet or a sling.

Clothing

One of the other key issues with preemies is that they need to be kept very, very warm because they have little or no body fat. At home, you want to dress them in two layers more than you ordinarily would, until they reach 7½ pounds. There are special clothes and diapers for premature babies because they're so tiny.

Sleep

Understand that your baby is going to sleep even more than a full-term baby because that's what he would have been doing in the womb—sleep, sleep, sleep. Sleep is the best thing your baby can do in the beginning to catch up. However, be prepared for your baby to sleep for shorter periods of time than full-term babies do.

Crying

Preemies may cry less than other babies because they don't have the physical strength. Instead, they may shut down more easily, so beware of overstimulation, or the opposite—you want to make sure they're getting proper stimulation.

Routines

Institute all the routines I suggest in Setting Firm Ground later than if your child were full-term. Later with scheduled feeds, later with solid food, later with sleep schedules. How much later depends on her size when born and how quickly she's catching up. To gauge it, go by her developmental age, not her chronological one. This is particularly important when adding solids because preemies may choke more easily and have immature digestive systems.

OTHER SPECIAL NEEDS BABIES

Because of prenatal tests, it's likely that if you have a special needs baby, you knew in advance. However, whether you were prepared or surprised, the most important thing to remember is that this is your baby. Just because he's been born differently from the "norm" doesn't mean that he should receive any less of your attention or love—if not more, because of his medical circumstances.

That's why I would make sure that above all, parents receive counseling, both to accept the medical condition that your child has been born with as well as support for the condition itself. I encourage you to find out everything that you possibly can do to make life as normal as possible.

Ask your doctor as many questions as you want, as many times as you need. Make note of the answers if need be. Ask if your child is eligible for an early support program and whether there is a child development center in your area that can help. Your doctor will know what services are available and if not, the Internet is full of resources. Ask if his condition will get better or worse over time. Find out as much info as you can.

Even if you knew what you were getting into, from day one, you'll be dealing with your emotions. Because it's one thing to know that your child has cystic fibrosis, multiple sclerosis, Down syndrome, spina bifida, or a congenital heart problem. And it's another thing to deal with it in reality. The reality hits, for instance, that your baby is not as responsive as he would be if he didn't have this condition.

There are really two kinds of extra work: the emotional work of acceptance, and the physical work of caring for a baby with special needs. You have to accept that "this is what my baby has," and then work on being the best parent that you possibly can and giving your baby the upbringing that she deserves.

So much of it has to do with your mind-set, your determination not to let your emotions tear you apart, but rather to find out all you can to give your child the very best. I've seen, for example, babies that have been born with Down syndrome who end up doing extremely well because of the incredible continuous care they received from their families.

That doesn't take away the very real demands of a child who's got special needs, because those are real. But take it on as a challenge to be faced, while making sure you're getting care and support as well, because you are going to be with other parents who have children that don't have medical conditions and you're not going to be able to help but compare. You'll look and think, "My child's not doing that." But you'll know why. And you know what *you* can do to give your child the maximum possible healthy and happy life.

Give yourself time to adjust to this new reality. If you find yourself becoming depressed, be sure to get help. Listen to those around you if they suggest you get support. Your doctor can be a source for a support group or a counselor. So can the resources in the back of this book. Be aware that you and your partner may be at different parts of the journey of acceptance. Listen to how one another feels, and get support as a couple if you need it. Find ways to have time together apart from the baby.

Dealing with Siblings

Having a baby with special needs can be quite difficult to explain to a young child. But it's not really necessary to explain because from his limited understanding, it's not any different from having a "normal" sibling.

If the sibling is older, you're able to explain more and they're better able to understand than a toddler. But of course it's a process. As the older sibling grows, he's able to recognize that his younger brother or sister needs more help.

And just like you, your older child will be able to develop more patience, more understanding, more empathy as a result of being part of your special family. They can end up developing good qualities that might not necessarily otherwise have come until adulthood. That's what makes this journey unique. But please be patient with your other children too, as they're learning as well.

Dealing with Other People

One of the challenges parents of special needs babies face is dealing with the comments and questions from others. Only you can find your way with this. Especially with strangers, don't feel obligated to go into a whole long explanation unless you feel like it. If people make remarks that offend you, walk away. You don't have to explain to anyone.

When it comes to family members, understand that they're going through their own process of acceptance also, and are asking questions out of concern for you and your child. If you know what you need from them in terms of support, ask. If they offend you, teach them how you want to be spoken to about the situation. This is an area in which being in a support group of people in a similar situation can really help.

One thing that can be challenging with a special needs baby is that if you can see her impairment, it is often easier than if you can't. That's because other people have expectations for these babies that they wouldn't have if they understood the difference.

◻

Above all, have a positive mind-set. Many of the families with special needs children that I know have found that their child really brings out the best in them. Parents surprise themselves with the understanding, compassion, and empathy they develop. It puts the rest of life into perspective. It takes someone special to raise a special needs child, and I know one day you'll look in the mirror and know that person is you!

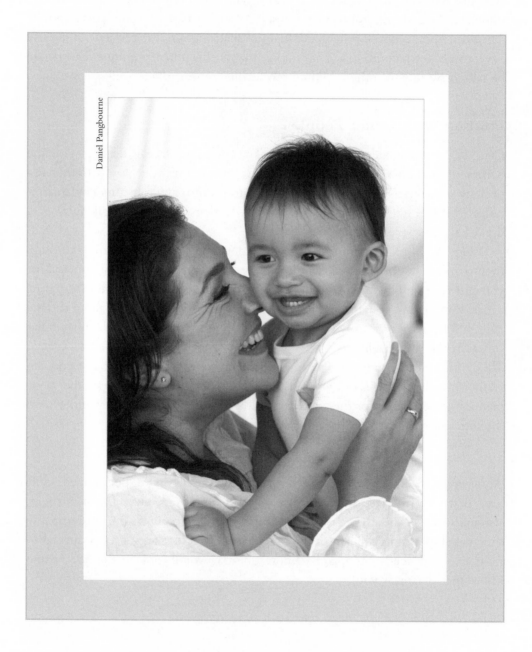

Daniel Pangbourne

CHAPTER 10

The Adopted Baby

ust like every other parent, you're finally holding the baby you've been waiting for. Just like every other parent, you're saying, "I am ready to take on the responsibility of being a loving parent and raising my child to be a loving human being."

I think I know a bit of what you're feeling because I've had a somewhat similar experience as a nanny. Some of the babies I've looked after are now teenagers, and I've never looked after any baby with any less moral responsibility, delight, nurturing, or loving than I would my own. And that's something that's really hard to explain. Because people always say, "Oh, well, when you've got your own, it's different." Maybe that's true for those who have to feel that babies have to biologically come from them.

But aren't babies a blessing, period? So I know you can love and care for your baby regardless of where he's biologically come from. More than anything, because of the whole elaborate adoption process, if there ever was a conscious decision to have a child, it was made by parents who adopt.

I also know that like other parents, you're going to worry about her health and well-being and about whether you're up to the job at times. Like them, you've got to work out feeding schedules and routines. Like them, you're going to feel emotional at times, because it isn't just pregnancy hormones that make you feel overwhelmed. Otherwise, how would fathers feel the same?

I know that like every parent, you want the best for your baby. Almost every word in this book applies to you. You're going to need as much patience, confidence, and love as any other parent. I've chosen to include this chapter to talk a bit about issues that I want you to think about based on the unique way your child came into your family. In particular, you need to take into account the age of the child and his history before making decisions about schedules, sleeping arrangements, and stimulation.

Getting Your Baby

There's one key difference between you and other parents. When you meet your baby, Mom's not as worn out as biological mothers. So you don't have that lack of energy and emotional tiredness as if you had given birth vaginally or gone through a C-section.

Instead, you're probably excited. You're ready for a little party. If your baby is newborn, you can easily overwhelm her with your energy, so be aware that she needs her rest. And remember that soon you're going to be hit by the fatigue too. Whether you're breast-feeding or you're bottle-feeding, you're still going to have to deal with those nights when your baby wakes up, wanting feeding on demand.

If your baby is older when he's adopted, he may be feeling confused or upset. Who is this new person who is holding him? Where is the person who has been caring for him? He may cry a lot in those first days and/or refuse one or the other of you. You may be afraid he won't love you. Don't worry—as you care for him, his connection to you will grow.

If possible, get as much information about his history before you adopted him, as well as any genetic or other medical information that may be relevant for his health as he grows. If it's not an open adoption, see if you can arrange a way to trace the birth parents if you ever need to for a health problem. If this isn't possible because your child was abandoned, remember that the need for such information is rare, so try not to worry too much about it. You just want to know as much as possible so you can do the best possible as a parent.

Bonding

Many adoptive parents get very anxious if they don't immediately connect to their baby. Actually, it has nothing to do with giving birth, as many biological parents who don't automatically bond with their babies will tell you. Just like biological parents, you may be swept away by a sea of emotions, creating waves of positive and negative feelings: fear, inadequacy, exhilaration, love, the realization that your life will never be the same. Understand that these are the feelings of parenthood, not because of the route you used to become parents.

As I said in earlier chapters, some people bond instantly; others need time for the relationship to develop. Don't scare yourself that it's about the fact that he's adopted. Whether you birthed them or not, babies come in with their own little ways of being, and might not be what you imagined. It's no different from biological parents who say, "Oh, I want a boy, and now I've got a girl." You grow in love over time with the one you have. If you continue to worry about this as the weeks and months go by, or feel that your child is not bonding to you, please get help from your doctor, who can refer you to the right support.

It's very easy as a parent to find excuses for why you're not bonding with your child if he's adopted. It's human instinct to come up with reasons why, especially when you've waited so many months to receive the baby that you have wanted so badly. The important thing here is just to respect that your little baby is unique and very, very special. In your own time, together you will bond. I say *in time* because that's exactly what it's going to take, time. No relationship bond is a deep one unless the time is put in to really connect.

Postnatal Depression

Yes, adoptive moms can become depressed. It may not have hormonal components, but the difference between your ideas of how you'll feel and the reality can trigger a downward spiral. You may experience feelings of inadequacy and overwhelmedness, anxiety, and maybe negative thoughts about yourself and your baby. It may physically manifest in sweats and heart palpitations, or feeling very lethargic. If you experience any of these or other unsettling feelings or thoughts, I would strongly advise that you talk to somebody close to you, and if that doesn't help, reach out and talk to a doctor or therapist. Because without help, you can spiral downward.

Dealing with Infertility

Many adoptive parents have had a tremendous number of tries to get pregnant before choosing adoption. So dealing with their infertility is a part of what a lot of adoptive parents must come to terms with. Some folks think they've dealt with their grief, only to feel it very strongly when they get their baby. Women, in particular, may feel sorrow that they haven't given birth to this child, or perhaps about not being there for the first months if your baby is older.

Why is it that you feel incomplete? Is it that you haven't experienced giving birth or gone through the stages of carrying a child? Hopefully you've reached an acceptance of that before the baby arrives, but if the feelings get stirred up again, do get support. Because this is what you've been waiting so long for—your baby is here, even if it didn't happen in the way you imagined.

Millions of families have been happily created by adoption. Feelings of infertility grief are a normal process for some parents. Understand that you're in a phase and get help, so that you can move on to the feelings of giving a child a place within your home and in your heart. Get moving with it so you can experience parenthood at its best.

Breast-feeding

These days, there is a trend toward adoptive mothers taking hormones in order to breast-feed their babies, or buying breast milk from others to give their newborns antibodies. It was well-known when I was born that my mother shared her abundant supply of breast milk to women in the ward who had none. So I say, Who am I to knock anyone who gets breast milk for their baby from someone else? Each and everyone to their own, really. The main thing here is do what's best for you, and don't judge another mother's decisions.

When it comes to injecting hormones, that's a decision that should be made only after advice from a doctor. What are the possible side effects of taking such hormones? I would also most definitely advise any woman considering such a step to talk to someone on the emotional level as well, to explore why she wants to make that choice. Millions of babies have done just fine on formula. Are you doing this for the baby, or for you?

Open Adoption

A lot of people have open adoptions in which the adoptive parents agree to stay in contact with the birth mother and/or father. If you're in this situation, be prepared for emotional times during the first year for both parties. It takes a level of maturity to do this properly. The well-being must be focused on the baby, not on the emotional needs of the adults. If you find that one of the adults is not on an even keel, then by all means have that open discussion so that person can get extra support. That is incredibly healthy not just for all the adults involved, but for the baby too.

It certainly is possible for open adoptions to work well. I know of a person who was a teenager when he had a baby, and now has a wonderful relationship with his daughter and is very close to her adoptive parents. Be sure everyone in the situation has support for making wise decisions and for going through their feelings.

Here are my suggestions for making open adoption work for everyone, especially your baby:

- Make sure your expectations of each other are clear.
- Establish what the child will call each person: Who gets to be called Mom and Dad? What will the others be called?
- If you don't have a written communication contract, it's a good idea to create a verbal one. It should spell out how often there will be communication, and in what form (letters, calls, photos, visits).
- The agreement should also spell out who else, if anyone, in the birth parents' families will also be in contact (grandmothers, fathers, etc.).

Be aware that you are entering into a relationship that will evolve over time. Many birth parents end up using the phone as the main mode of communication. They want to hear about how the baby is doing, but are uncomfortable around the adoptive family because of unresolved feelings. Adoptive parents, on the other hand, may feel threatened by the birth parents, feeling less "real," and will look for ways to distance themselves. Some birth parents disappear after a couple of years; some stay connected forever. You will have to work many things out as you go along, keeping the needs of the child left, right, and center. Be prepared to continue to make mutually-agreed-upon decisions.

Some periods may be easy, others challenging. As in any relationship, you will learn what to expect from one another, and discover more and more about what works best for you all.

Surrogates

I feel strongly that people who use surrogate mothers and gay people who have women bear children for them (or have friends as sperm donors) be clear about the specifics of keeping an open relationship. Again, the well-being of the child should come first, and my suggestions regarding open adoption apply here too.

Adopting a Baby of a Different Nationality

In the first year, any issues of nationality are totally irrelevant to your baby. But you do have to be prepared. You have to understand that you're now a biracial family, and that has implications for you and your child in the future— wonderful and positive implications. Your baby's heritage will encourage you to research another culture, just as you would if you married someone of a differ- ent nationality. In the first year, however, the only thing that matters is under- standing that you may need to take care of her hair, for example, in a different way than you know, depending on what her nationality is.

Institutionalized Children

Many children, especially those adopted from abroad in places like Russia, Ro- mania, China, Vietnam, and Cambodia, have been institutionalized before being adopted, and may be delayed physically, emotionally, and intellectually as a result of neglect. These infants are generally not adopted as newborns, but at six, nine, or twelve months. These babies may have been starved. If that's true, it's impor- tant to give small quantities of food at very frequent intervals so she doesn't de- velop bad habits like hoarding food.

It's also important for you to know if your baby's delayed so that you can get going on bringing her up to square one. Even if you don't know her history, you can tell from significant physical, emotional, or mental delays. Generally, neglected children are undersized and seriously behind in development.

If your baby is delayed, you need to step back a bit, as if you're dealing with a preemie. For instance, if you adopt a child who's a year old, if her development is behind, you go back and parent as if she's much younger. Her calendar age is less important than her developmental age. Even more than with other babies, what's important is that you're seeing progress, not how she compares to others on a chart.

As the parent of an abandoned or neglected baby, your job is to make him feel incredibly safe and secure so that he can trust you. Because with trust, he'll start to connect emotionally with you and then start to explore the stimulations you place in front of him. This gives him the competence to reach those milestones.

The most important thing, as it is with any baby, is creating those harmonic times where you and your child are enjoying yourselves. You're both laughing and enjoying the stimulating play, whether it's creating body awareness or eye-hand coordination, or developing listening skills or visual tracking. The fact that you're doing it with her is what's significant.

As a parent, what matters to you the most is feeling a great determination to get your baby back on track. It's like you're coaching her on that mile-long run so she can end up on the finish line. I encourage you to see it as a very exciting rather than a fearful thing: "Okay, I'm going marshal all my love and all my attention to give her a boost up!" Focus and commit 100 percent to bring your child up to scratch.

Adapting My Advice from Other Chapters

During the first year, the baby's "job" is to develop a sense of basic trust in the world. This trust develops through the bond, or attachment, she makes with her caregivers. As a result of interruptions in this bonding process, especially in cases of abuse and/or neglect, some adopted children develop attachment problems. Symptoms in infants are either babies who are too good—they never make demands and rarely cry, and are content to entertain themselves for hours—or babies who are inconsolable and reject comforting from parents, don't make eye contact, or don't imitate parents. If your baby is exhibiting such symptoms after the first month or so, be sure to see an attachment specialist or family therapist. You can find one through your adoption agency. Or talk to your doctor.

To minimize the possibility of attachment problems, especially if your child was abandoned or neglected, I would recommend the following modifications to my advice in other chapters:

- Consider keeping your baby next to you in a crib or a co-sleeper (one of those things that attach to the side of your bed) longer than other infants. She will get great comfort from your physical presence.
- Keep him on you in a sling more than you might otherwise.
- I would not use the controlled crying technique. Often these babies were abandoned at night, so sleeping is challenging. Under the circumstances, if she cries, pick her up and soothe her, no matter how many times. Eventually she'll feel safe.
- Your baby may experience night terrors—screaming, kicking, and thrashing while asleep—as a result of trauma. Again, pick her up and soothe her as best as possible. One thing that works is to wake her up, reassure her, and then put her down again.

Babies who have been abandoned and neglected need you to spend as much one-to-one time with them as possible. You have to really gain your baby's trust because she's been in care before where that trust has been broken. That's what you're doing here. You're creating a safe haven for your child so that she feels she can totally depend on you and trust the stability of your care. Dancing with your baby, doing massage, rolling her across an inflatable ball, lifting her up high to touch something, doing the famous Superman flying through the air. All of those activities allow your child to understand that she can trust you to hold her. Of course, all the peekaboo games should come a lot later because of the insecurity of being left.

Above all, the best thing you can give your infant is consistent caring that will show your child she can count on your love and depend on you to meet her needs. And that's no different than what all parents should be doing!

Talking about Adoption

The time is long past when the advice was to hide from your child the fact that she was adopted. As an infant, she of course can't understand. That doesn't really kick in until at least four. But many parents worry even when their child is an infant about when and how to discuss it. I believe you'll feel in your heart when it's the right time. And that's not until your child is a little older. Live in the moment and enjoy this first year of having your baby. That's what you should be focusing on now.

You can set the stage for a positive experience by talking to your little one right from the start about the day you met her and by creating a scrapbook that details your adoption journey, how you came together and what you as parents were feeling, just like birth parents do.

This scrapbook will be a little treasure chest when he becomes older. Rest assured that it will become one of your child's favorite books! It's one thing that all children like to hear as they get older: how their parents met and where they were from. These stories help to really allow a child to answer important questions: How do I fit in? Where is my place?

Support Groups

One of the realities about adoption is that it doesn't matter to you, but it does to your child. This is not relevant in the first year, but is something you need to be aware of right at the start. For you, it may be an unbelievably positive experience. But someday your child will understand what adoption means, and will have ambivalence about it that you don't have.

This doesn't mean he won't love you as much. But he will begin to think things like, "How come my birth parents didn't want me? There must be something wrong with me." And if it isn't an open adoption, "Who am I biologically? And what are my birth parents like?"

While these thoughts and feelings are down the line for your child, one of the best things you can do right from the start is be in a support group of parents and children in similar situations, so all of you can find like-minded people to connect with. There are lots of organizations of families with babies from around the world that you can get together with. Try your adoption agency for starters. You want to be able to get the best knowledge, support, and suggestions that you can.

Above all, though, just as I say throughout this book, please relish this wonderful time with your new baby! Getting her off to a good start will go a long way to creating a solid parent-child relationship that will be your joy—and hers.

PART IV

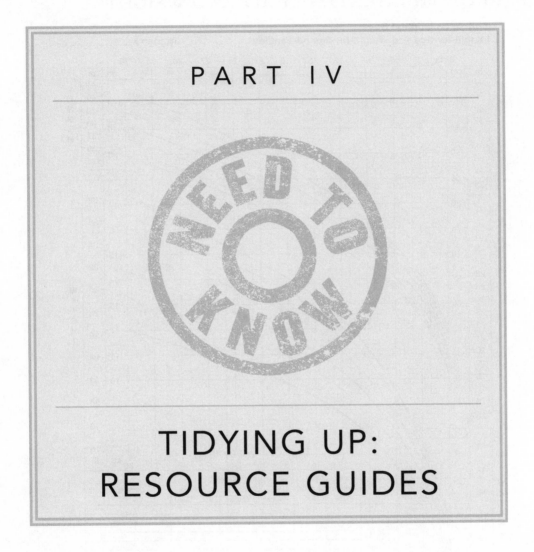

TIDYING UP:
RESOURCE GUIDES

GROWTH CHARTS: HEIGHT AND WEIGHT

Birth to 36 months: Boys
Length-for-age and Weight-for-age percentiles

NAME _____

RECORD # _____

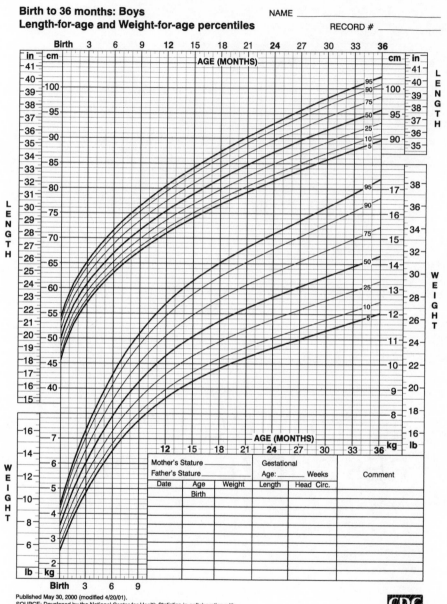

Published May 30, 2000 (modified 4/20/01).
SOURCE: Developed by the National Center for Health Statistics in collaboration with
the National Center for Chronic Disease Prevention and Health Promotion (2000).
http://www.cdc.gov/growthcharts

SAFER · HEALTHIER · PEOPLE™

Birth to 36 months: Girls
Length-for-age and Weight-for-age percentiles

NAME _____

RECORD # _____

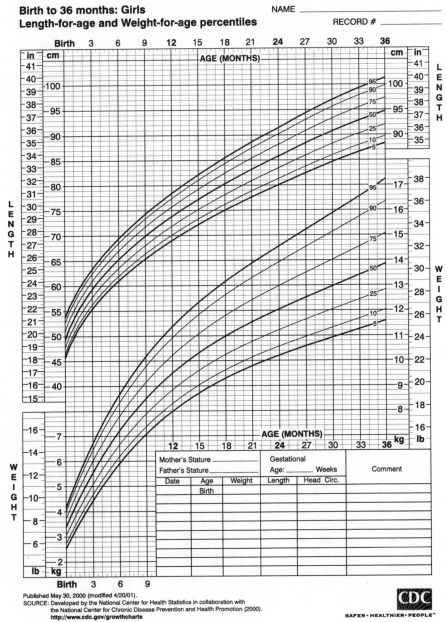

Published May 30, 2000 (modified 4/20/01).
SOURCE: Developed by the National Center for Health Statistics in collaboration with
the National Center for Chronic Disease Prevention and Health Promotion (2000).
http://www.cdc.gov/growthcharts

CDC

SAFER • HEALTHIER • PEOPLE™

U.S. Centers for Disease Control and Prevention
Recommended Immunization Schedule
for First Year
For the best schedule for your child, consult your child's physician.

Child's Age	Vaccine and Dose	Protects Against
At Birth	Hepatitis B Dose 1 of 3	Hepatitis B virus (chronic inflammation of the liver, lifelong complications)
1–2 months	Hepatitis B Dose 2 of 3	Hepatitis B virus (chronic inflammation of the liver, lifelong complications)
2 months (part of well-baby visit)	DTaP Dose 1 of 5	Diphtheria, tetanus, and pertussis (whooping cough)
	Hib Dose 1 of 4	Infections of the blood, brain, joints, or lungs (pneumonia)
	Polio (IPV) Dose 1 of 4	Polio
	Pneumococcal conjugate (PCV7) Dose 1 of 4	Infections of the blood, brain, joints, inner ears, or lungs (pneumonia)
	Rotavirus Dose 1 of 3	Rotavirus diarrhea (and vomiting)
4 months (part of well-baby visit)	DTaP Dose 2 of 5	Diphtheria, tetanus, and pertussis (whooping cough)
	Hib Dose 2 of 4	Infections of the blood, brain, joints, or lungs (pneumonia)
	Polio (IPV) Dose 2 of 4	Polio
	Pneumococcal conjugate (PCV7) Dose 2 of 4	Infections of the blood, brain, joints, inner ears, or lungs (pneumonia)
	Rotavirus Dose 2 of 3	Rotavirus diarrhea (and vomiting) .

Child's Age	Vaccine and Dose	Protects Against
6 months (part of well-baby visit)	DTaP Dose 3 of 5	Diphtheria, tetanus and pertussis (whooping cough)
	Hib Dose 3 of 4	Infections of the blood, brain, joints, or lungs (pneumonia)
	Pneumococcal conjugate (PCV7) Dose 3 of 4	Infections of the blood, brain, joints, inner ears, or lungs (pneumonia)
	Rotavirus Dose 3 of 3	Rotavirus diarrhea (and vomiting)
6–18 months	Hepatitis B Dose 3 of 3	Hepatitis B (chronic inflammation of the liver, lifelong complications)
	Polio (IPV) Dose 3 of 4	Polio
6 months or older	Influenza Dose 1 of 2	Flu and complications
	Influenza Dose 2 of 2	Flu and complications

COMMON ILLNESSES AND AILMENTS IN BABIES

The following chart is by no means a comprehensive guide, just a heads-up to common illnesses you might encounter. I recommend getting a good infant medical care book that gives more details and treatment suggestions. See doctor unless otherwise indicated.

ILLNESS/AILMENT	SYMPTOMS	ACTION
Acne	small red bumps on the skin that appear shortly after birth	Will clear up
Asthma: recurring coughing and wheezing	coughing, rapid breathing, rapid movement of the muscles below the ribs, flaring of nostrils, wheezing, bluish tint to lips or nails	Call the doctor
Bronchiolitis: infection of the smaller passages of the lungs	runny nose, mild cough, fever; then after a couple of days the cough becomes worse and breathing labored	Call the doctor
Cold	runny nose, mild cough, sometimes fever	Use a humidifier. Call the doctor if fever rises above 100.4°F (38°C)
Conjunctivitis: also known as pinkeye or sticky eye	swelling, redness, discharge in the eye(s)	If newborn, call the doctor immediately as it is very contagious and can be linked to pneumonia
Cradle cap	scaly patches on the scalp	Will clear up
Croup: inflammation of the voice box and windpipe	a whistling or barking sound when breathing or coughing; struggles to breathe, turns blue when coughs	Call the doctor
Diarrhea	loose stools more than 6–8 times a day	Call the doctor
Ear infection: infection of the inner tubes of the ear	irritability, especially at night; may pull or bat at ear; fever	Call the doctor
Eczema	reddish skin that oozes and becomes scaly, caused by allergy or contact with something irritating	Call the doctor
Fever	high temperaure, sweating	Call the doctor if it rises above 100.4°C (38°C)
Flu	dry cough, sudden fever, chills and shakes	Call the doctor if fever rises above 100.4°C (38°C)
Gastroesophageal reflux	vomits after eating	Burp often and keep upright for 30 minutes after feeding;

ILLNESS/AILMENT	SYMPTOMS	ACTION
		see a doctor if it's excessive or persistent
Heat rash	small bumps that appear when exposed to sun or heat	Keep cool and dry; apply calamine lotion
Heat stroke	dangerous! suddenly raised temperature due to getting too hot, e.g., on the beach, in the car, being overdressed in hot, humid weather. CAN CAUSE DEATH	Cool body down ASAP (undress, sponge or wet with cool water) and CALL AN AMBULANCE OR GO TO EMERGENCY ROOM
Hives	itchy red, raised bumps that look like welts, either all over the body or in one area; may be caused by allergic reaction to food, pollen, drugs, insect stings, or infection	Call the doctor
Impetigo	bacterial infection of the eyelid; highly contagious	Call the doctor
Ingrown nail	redness around the nail	Call the doctor
Jaundice	yellowing of the skin	Will clear up if mild; if it persists, see a doctor: may need a sunlamp for a few days
Pneumonia: a viral or bacterial lung infection	cough, rapid breathing, rapid movement of the muscles below the ribs, flaring of nostrils, wheezing, bluish tint to lips or nails	Call the doctor
Seizure	shaking of whole body/part of body	Call the doctor
Thrush	white patches in the mouth, redness of throat, baby off their milk	Call the doctor
Vomiting		If excessive, projectile, accompanied by fever or diarrhea, or goes on for more than 12 hours, call the doctor immediately. Dehydration may occur, which can be fatal

MENINGITIS

Is your baby getting worse, fast? Babies can become ill very quickly, so remember to check them often. Not every baby gets all these symptoms, and they can appear in any order.

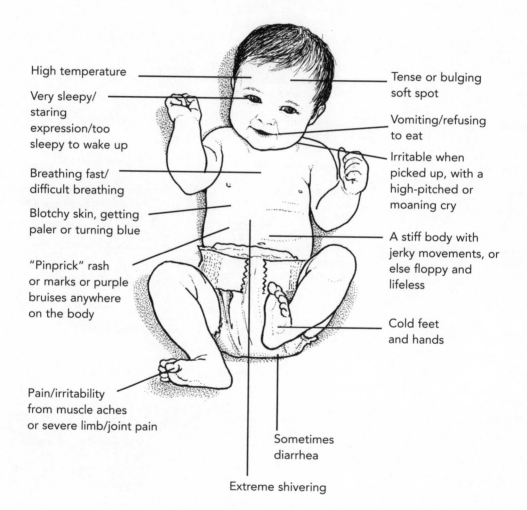

High temperature

Very sleepy/ staring expression/too sleepy to wake up

Breathing fast/ difficult breathing

Blotchy skin, getting paler or turning blue

"Pinprick" rash or marks or purple bruises anywhere on the body

Pain/irritability from muscle aches or severe limb/joint pain

Tense or bulging soft spot

Vomiting/refusing to eat

Irritable when picked up, with a high-pitched or moaning cry

A stiff body with jerky movements, or else floppy and lifeless

Cold feet and hands

Sometimes diarrhea

Extreme shivering

EMERGENCY FIRST AID FOR CHILDREN UNDER ONE

I strongly recommend every parent take an emergency first aid and CPR class. I'm including the basics here as a reminder only, not as a substitute for proper training. Reading about CPR is very different than performing it.

Rule number one in any emergency: stay calm, call for emergency help, and stay with your child.

Burns

- Run cool water, not cold, over burn until pain subsides, up to twenty minutes.
- If first degree (redness, slight swelling, no blistering, major swelling, or charring), apply gauze dressing.
- If second or third degree (blistering, a lot of swelling, or charring), caused by electricity or chemicals, is on face or eyes, leave uncovered and go to the hospital.
- Do not immerse baby in cold water.
- Do not remove clothing.

Cuts or Scrapes

- Hold under cool running water.
- Remove any dirt with clean tweezers under running water.
- Apply pressure with gauze until bleeding subsides. If blood seeps through gauze, add another piece on top.
- Dress with antibiotic cream and cover with bandage.
- If the cut is deep or bleeding, doesn't stop quickly, or you can't get the dirt out, get emergency help.

Choking

- If coughing, crying, or breathing, do nothing. Do not offer fluids. They may block air passage more.

- If not breathing, call ambulance immediately and:
  - Place your baby facedown on your knees and push rapidly and firmly five times with the heel of your hand between his shoulder blades to expel object.
  - If that doesn't work, put him on his back on the floor and, using two fingers, press his chest at the breastbone five times in quick succession, about a half-inch deep, being careful not to injure his rib cage. (See diagram of infant CPR)

Heat Stroke

- Take baby to a cool place and remove clothes. Bring down temperature immediately with cool sponge bath or immersion in cool bathwater and fanning while calling for emergency help.

Head Injury

- If it's a tumble that produces a small knot (egghead bruise), an ice pack should do the trick.
- If you suspect a serious head injury or an injury to the spine, do not move your baby. Call ambulance immediately. Stabilize while waiting for help by placing your hands on either side of the baby to keep head still.
- If baby is throwing up, roll whole body over to prevent choking and protect neck and spine.
- If she's unconscious, check to see if she's breathing. If not, administer CPR while waiting for ambulance. (See Infant CPR box on pp. 227–28)
- If there's bleeding, apply pressure with a diaper or other cloth until bleeding stops. Then apply ice pack to reduce swelling. Heavy bleeding from the scalp does not necessarily mean a serious wound, because there are lots of blood vessels close to the surface. However, if you can't stop the bleeding or it's severe, call the ambulance.
- If you suspect a skull fracture, do not apply pressure.
- If skin is broken and dirt is in wound, do not clean. Cover with gauze and seek immediate medical attention, as head wounds can cause brain infections.

- If eyes are crossed, or one pupil is dilated more than the other, or he's been unconscious even briefly, get emergency help immediately.
- For twenty-four hours after any head injury, your baby should be monitored for unconsciousness, vomiting, or trouble breathing. To be on the safe side, consult your doctor. You may be advised to wake her every few hours to make sure she's not unconscious.

INFANT CPR

If your baby is unconscious, call for emergency help and check for responsiveness by tapping gently on chest, shoulders or feet. If you get no response, do ABC:

1. **Airway:** Quickly check to see if he's breathing—look, listen, and feel for signs of breathing. If not, tilt head back so nose is pointed up. Be careful not to put head too far back as this can block the air passage in infants. (See left figure on following page.)
2. **Breathing:** Cover the baby's mouth and nose with your mouth, creating a seal. Gently and quickly give a puff of air, then remove your mouth and watch and listen for an exhale. (See middle figure on following page.) If none, repeat one breath, covering his nose and mouth. If he's still unresponsive, check:
3. **Circulation:** Place two of your fingers for 3–5 seconds at the brachial artery, which is located inside of his upper arm, between the elbow and the shoulder. If you do not feel a pulse within that time, then his heart is not beating, and you will need to do chest compressions.
4. **Compression:** Place two fingers on the breastbone—just below the nipples. Make sure not to press at the very end of the breastbone. Keep your other hand on the infant's forehead, keeping the head tilted back. Press down on the infant's chest so that it compresses about one-third to one-half the depth of the chest. (See right figure on following page.) Press gently but firmly; you can easily damage the rib cage if you press too hard. Give thirty chest compressions. Each time, let the chest rise completely. These compressions should be

fast and hard with no pausing. Count the thirty compressions quickly. Then give the infant two breaths. The chest should rise. Continue CPR (*thirty* chest compressions followed by *two* breaths, then repeat) for about two minutes.

5. After about two minutes of CPR, if the infant still does not have normal breathing, coughing, or any movement, leave the infant if you are alone and call 911. Then continue CPR (thirty chest compressions followed by two breaths, then repeat) until the infant recovers or help arrives. If the infant starts breathing again, place him or her in the recovery position. Periodically re-check for breathing until help arrives.

Insect Stings

- Apply cool compress until pain subsides.
- Remove stinger by scraping it with a credit card. Do not use tweezers, as this may force it farther in.
- Watch for infection: streaks of red or yellow, or signs of allergic reaction:
  Unconsciousness
  Difficulty breathing
  Hives or itching over entire body
  Swelling of eyes, lips, or penis

Poisoning

- Take away the substance and remove any from mouth. Save for analysis.
- If she's drooling, sleepy, having trouble breathing or convulsing, call ambulance immediately.
- Otherwise, call poison control center, describe symptoms, and follow their instructions.

FIRST AID KIT

Here are what I consider essentials for the first year and beyond:

- antibiotic cream for scrapes and cuts
- cotton wool
- Fever reducers like infant Motrin or Tylenol. Be sure to consult doctor before giving, especially to babies under three months. Never give aspirin to children as it is linked to a serious liver disorder called Reye's syndrome.
- first aid manual
- gauze dressings to clean cuts and stop bleeding and adhesive tape to hold in place
- hand sanitizer
- hydrogen peroxide for disinfecting cuts
- ice pack—small and large. The new flexible ones that don't require freezing are great. Just twist and they're cold.
- oral syringe or droppers for giving medicine
- plasters in various sizes
- rehydrating fluids like Pedialyte in case of infant diarrhea
- rubbing alcohol for disinfecting tweezers, and tweezers for removing splinters, glass, etc.
- small scissors
- thermometer—digital rectal

TOYS FOR THE FIRST YEAR

- musical games and toys
- shape/numbers/animal sorters
- stacking rings/stacking cups/blocks
- cloth or plastic playhouses that go over a table
- role-play equipment: pots and pans/dustpan/brush
- pull and push toys like dogs and caterpillars on leashes, activity walkers
- large wooden knob floor puzzles
- drawing with finger paints and finger crayons (if very advanced)

- books, especially cloth and board
- press and turn toys/push-down spinning tops
- soft balls
- inflatable balls to lean on
- cuddly toys
- Tupperware/plastic bowls/big wooden spoons
- finger puppets
- activity train sets
- dolls

- boxes
- bath toys
- buckets
- plastic keys/cell phones
- plastic telephones
- rides/wooden bikes
- cushions
- bubbles
- colored scarves
- mirrors
- tunnels
- YOU

USEFUL RESOURCES

Adoption

Adoption Information Resource List
American Academy of Pediatrics
www.aap.org

Adoptive Families of America
(800) 372-3300
www.adoptivefamilies.com

Advice and Support

www.jofrost.com
My Web site, where you can ask me questions, share your learnings with other parents worldwide, and get support.

A Healthy Me
www.ahealthyme.com
All kinds of information on infancy and parenting.

Baby Center
www.babycenter.com
Track your baby's development online and much more.

LoveToKnow Baby
www.baby.lovetoknow.com
Share what you're learning about your baby with other mothers and fathers. Lots of resources for adoptive parents here too.

Breast-feeding

Breastfeeding.com
www.breastfeeding.com
"Information, support and attitude!"

La Leche League
www.Illi.org
This organization has been supporting breast-feeding moms for decades, and offers mom-to-mom forums and referrals to local lactation specialists.

Child Care

Child Care Aware
www.childcareaware.org
Offers referrals by zip code, as well as loads of helpful tools and information, including a cost calculator for a variety of options.

Child Care Resources Inc.
www.childcareresourcesinc.org
Go here for referrals to qualified programs as well as information about financial aid.

Dads

Here are two online communities for expectant and new fathers:

Brand New Dad
www.brandnewdad.com

Dads Adventure
www.newdads.com

Diapers

Diaper Pin
www.diaperpin.com
Information about cloth diapers and the new cloth ones with disposable inserts.

1-800-Diapers
www.1800diapers.com
Buy disposable diapers online, as well as baby detergent, wipes, rash ointment, formula, and other baby supplies.

Doulas

DONA International
www.dona.org
Offers information about what birth and postnatal doulas do and how to find one anywhere in the world.

Grandparents

AARP
www.aarp.org
This organization for those fifty-five and older has a wide variety of grandparenting resources.

Grandparents Magazine
www.grandparentsmagazine.net
Online articles and resources, including song lyrics.

GRANDtimes
www.grandtimes.com
Lots of tips and articles.

Health Concerns

Baby Health Center
www.mayoclinic.com/health/healthy-baby/
FL99999
This service of the Mayo Clinic has all kinds of health information about babies.

Infant Health Center
www.keepkidshealthy.com/infant/infant.html
All kinds of health info and parenting advice on everything from food allergies to how to figure out how sick your child is.

Multiple Births

http://dmoz.org/Home/Family/Multiple
_Births/Parenting/
This list offers dozens of links to multiple Web sites.

Nannies

Here are four Web sites for nanny and other one-on-one care:
www.nannies4hire.com
www.aupaircare.com

www.nanny-agency.com
www.greatnannies.com

Postpartum Depression

Family Doctor.org
familydoctor.org/379.xml
Extensive information about postpartum depression symptoms and treatment.

PPD Support Group
www.ppdsupportpage.com
Women supporting women online.

Postpartum Support International
www.postpartum.net
You can find resources and support here, including individual support in your geographic area.

Preemies

www.preemies.org
Offers resources and chat rooms for parents with babies in the neonatal intensive care unit and beyond.

www.prematurity.org
Has links to lots of resources and research.

www.preemie.info
Lots of photos and stories, as well as resources.

Safety

BabyProofingPlus.com
www.babyproofingplus.com
Hundreds of safety products in one Web site.

Home Safety Services
www.homesafety.net
Lots of information and checklists, as well as a place to ask your safety questions.

Special Needs

BellaOnline
www.bellaonline.com/articles/art50678.asp
For mothers, by mothers of special needs children. Includes links to all kinds of resources.

Matrix Parent Network and Resource Center
www.matrixparents.org/links.html
Provides links to all kinds of help for special needs children.

Special Babies
http://carloperez.com/sb/chapter1.html
A guide for parents of special needs infants.

BABY LOG

This is a place for you to record all the little things your baby does that you'll want to remember—such as when they sleep, feed, wet their diaper. This log will be helpful to look back on . . .

_____

_____

_____

_____

_____

_____

_____

_____

_____

_____

_____

_____

_____

_____

_____

_____

_____

_____

_____

_____

_____

_____

_____

_____

_____

_____

Index